Editor
Lorin Klistoff, M.A.

Managing Editor
Karen J. Goldfluss, M.S. Ed.

Illustrator
Teacher Created Resources Staff

Cover Artist
Brenda DiAntonis

Art Production Manager
Kevin Barnes

Art Coordinator
Renée Christine Yates

Imaging
James Edward Grace
Rosa C. See

Publisher
Mary D. Smith, M.S. Ed.

DAILY WARM-UPS

Math

GRADE 2

- Over 300 daily math warm-ups
- Includes practice in five key areas:
  - Numbers and Numeration
  - Operations
  - Measurement and Geometry
  - Graphs, Data, and Probability
  - Algebra, Patterns, and Functions
- Ideal for review and test preparation!

Author

Heath Roddy

Teacher Created Resources, Inc.
6421 Industry Way
Westminster, CA 92683
www.teachercreated.com

ISBN-1-4206-3960-9

©2006 Teacher Created Resources, Inc.

Made in U.S.A.

Table of Contents

Table of Contents

Introduction

The *Daily Warm-Ups: Math* series was written to provide students with frequent opportunities to master and retain important math skills. The unique format used in this series provides students with the opportunity to improve their own fluency in math. Each section consists of at least 30 pages of challenging problems that meet national and state standards. (See Table of Contents to find a listing of specific subject areas. Answer keys are located at the back of each section.) Use the tracking sheet on page 6 to record which warm-up exercises you have given to your students. Or, distribute copies of the sheet for students to keep their own records.

This book is divided into five sections. The sections are as follows:

- Numbers and Numeration
- Operations
- Measurement and Geometry
- Graphs, Data and Probability
- Algebra, Patterns and Functions

Daily Warm-Ups: Math gives students a year-long collection of challenging problems to reinforce key math skills taught in the classroom. As students become active learners in discovering mathematical relationships, they acquire a necessary understanding that improves their problem-solving skills and, therefore, boosts their confidence in math. When using this book, keep the idea of incorporating the warm-ups with the actual curriculum that you may be currently using in your classroom. This provides students with a greater chance of mastering the math skills.

This book can be used in a variety of ways. However, the exercises in this book were designed to be used as warm-ups where students will have the opportunity to work problems and obtain immediate feedback from their teacher. To help ensure student success, spend a few moments each day discussing problems and solutions. This extra time will not take very long and will yield great results from students! As you use this book, you will be excited to watch your students discover how exciting math concepts can be!

Teaching Tips

Ideas on how to use the warm-ups are as follows:

- *Discussion*—Most warm-ups can be completed in a short amount of time. When time is up, model how to correctly work the problems. You may wish to have students correct their own work. Allow time for students to discuss problems and their solutions to problems. You may want to allow students the opportunity to discuss their answers or the way they solved the problems with partners. Discuss why some answers are correct and why others are not. Students should be able to support their choices. Having students understand that there are many ways of approaching a problem and strategies used in dealing with them are a great benefit for all students. The time you allow students to do this is just as important as the time spent completing the problems.

- *Review*—Give students the warm-up at the end of the lesson as a means of tying in an objective taught that day. The problems students encounter on each warm-up are designed to improve math fluency and are not intended to be included as a math grade. If the student has difficulty with an objective, then review the material again with him or her independently and provide additional instruction.

Introduction

Teaching Tips *(cont.)*

- *Assessment*—The warm-ups can be used as a preliminary assessment to find out what your students know. Use the assessment to tailor your lessons.
- *Introduction*—Use the warm-ups as an introduction into the new objective to be taught. Select warm-ups according to the specific skill or skills to be introduced. The warm-ups do not have to be distributed in any particular order.
- *Independent Work*—Photocopy the warm-up for students to work on independently.
- *Transparencies*—Make overhead transparencies for each lesson. Present each lesson as a means of introducing an objective not previously taught, or have students work off the transparency.
- *Model*—Invite students to come to the board to model how they approached a problem on the warm-up.
- *Test Preparation*—The warm-ups can be a great way to prepare for math tests in the classroom or for any standardized testing. You may wish to select warm-ups from all sections to use as practice tests and/or review prior to standardized testing.

Student Tips

Below is a chart that you may photocopy and cut out for each student. It will give students a variety of strategies to use when dealing with difficult problems.

✂ -

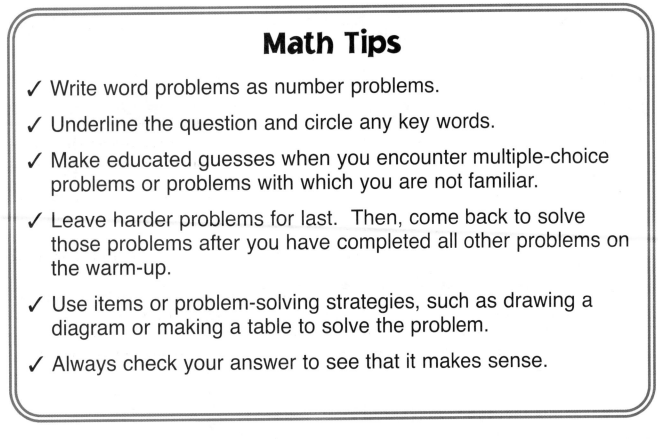

Math Tips

✓ Write word problems as number problems.

✓ Underline the question and circle any key words.

✓ Make educated guesses when you encounter multiple-choice problems or problems with which you are not familiar.

✓ Leave harder problems for last. Then, come back to solve those problems after you have completed all other problems on the warm-up.

✓ Use items or problem-solving strategies, such as drawing a diagram or making a table to solve the problem.

✓ Always check your answer to see that it makes sense.

Numbers and Numeration Warm-Ups

1	✓	8		15		22		29		36		43		50		57	
2	✓	9		16		23		30		37		44		51		58	
3	✓	10		17		24		31		38		45		52		59	✓
4	✓	11		18		25		32		39		46		53		60	✓
5	✓	12		19		26		33		40		47		54		61	
6		13		20		27		34		41		48		55		62	
7		14		21		28		35		42		49		56			

Operations Warm-Ups

1		8		15		22		29		36		43		50		57	
2		9		16		23		30		37		44		51		58	
3		10		17		24		31		38		45		52		59	
4		11		18		25		32		39		46		53		60	
5		12		19		26		33		40		47		54		61	
6		13		20		27		34		41		48		55		62	
7		14		21		28		35		42		49		56			

Measurement and Geometry Warm-Ups

1		8		15		22		29		36		43		50		57	
2		9		16		23		30		37		44		51		58	
3		10		17		24		31		38		45		52		59	
4		11		18		25		32		39		46		53		60	
5		12		19		26		33		40		47		54		61	
6		13		20		27		34		41		48		55		62	
7		14		21		28		35		42		49		56			

Graphs, Data and Probability Warm-Ups

1		8		15		22		29		36		43		50		57	
2		9		16		23		30		37		44		51		58	
3		10		17		24		31		38		45		52		59	
4		11		18		25		32		39		46		53		60	
5		12		19		26		33		40		47		54		61	
6		13		20		27		34		41		48		55		62	
7		14		21		28		35		42		49		56			

Algebra, Patterns and Functions Warm-Ups

1		8		15		22		29		36		43		50		57	
2		9		16		23		30		37		44		51		58	
3		10		17		24		31		38		45		52		59	
4		11		18		25		32		39		46		53		60	
5		12		19		26		33		40		47		54		61	
6		13		20		27		34		41		48		55		62	
7		14		21		28		35		42		49		56			

NUMBERS AND NUMERATION

DAILY Warm-Up 1

Name _____ Date _____

1. Look at the calculator. If you add 30 to the total, what would the display then read? *(Circle the correct letter.)*

   A. 63

   B. 73

   C. 83

   D. 90

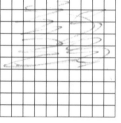

2. Jerry has one hundred sixty buttons. Shade in the number of buttons Jerry has on the model below. (*Use your pencil.*)

DAILY Warm-Up 2

Name _____ Date _____

1. Write the number below in words on the lines.

Hundreds	Tens	Ones
1	4	8

One Hundred
Forty Eight
_____

2. If you add 20 to the number below, what would be the new number? Write the new number in words on the lines.

Hundreds	Tens	Ones
1	7	8

198
_____
_____
_____

DAILY
Warm-Up 3

Name _____ Date _____

1. How many crayons are shown below? Write the answer as a multiplication problem on the line.

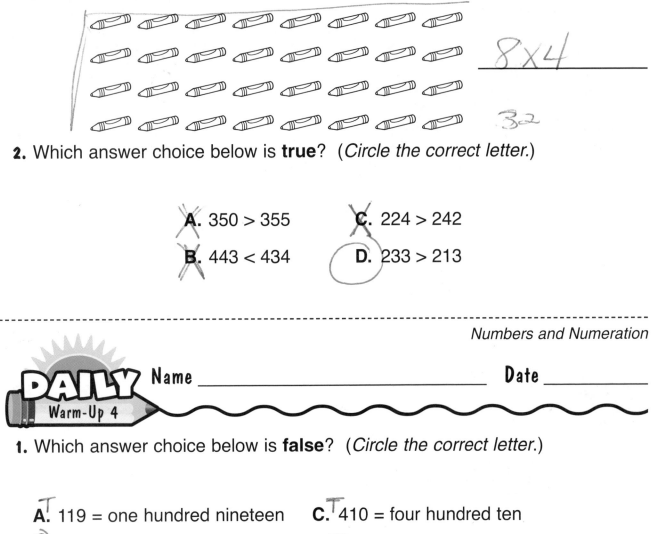

8×4

32

2. Which answer choice below is **true**? (*Circle the correct letter.*)

~~**A.** 350 > 355~~   ~~**C.** 224 > 242~~

~~**B.** 443 < 434~~   **D.** 233 > 213 ⟵ circled

DAILY
Warm-Up 4

Name _____ Date _____

1. Which answer choice below is **false**? (*Circle the correct letter.*)

A. 119 = one hundred nineteen ᵀ   **C.** 410 = four hundred ten ᵀ

B. 223 = two hundred twenty-six ⟵ circled, F   **D.** 387 = three hundred eighty-seven ᵀ

2. Margaret is counting her money. She has 7 one-dollar bills and 8 ten-dollar bills. Use the chart below to show how much money Margaret has.

Hundreds	Tens	Ones
	$8	7

DAILY **Warm-Up 5** Name _____ Date _____

1. Write the number of phones on the place value chart. *32*

Hundreds	Tens	Ones
	3	2

2. Which number below is equal to **two hundred seventy-six**? (*Circle the correct letter.*)

A. 267   **C.** 76

B. 276   **D.** 176

DAILY **Warm-Up 6** Name _____ Date _____

1. Which answer is **not** a correct way to show the number twenty-six? (*Circle the correct letter.*)

A.   **B.**   **C.**   **D.**

2. What fraction of the circle is shaded? (*Write the answer on the line.*)

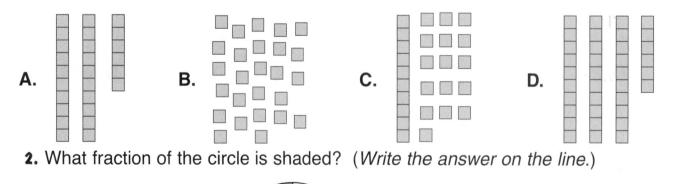

_____

DAILY
Warm-Up 7

Name _____ Date _____

1. Solve the problem.

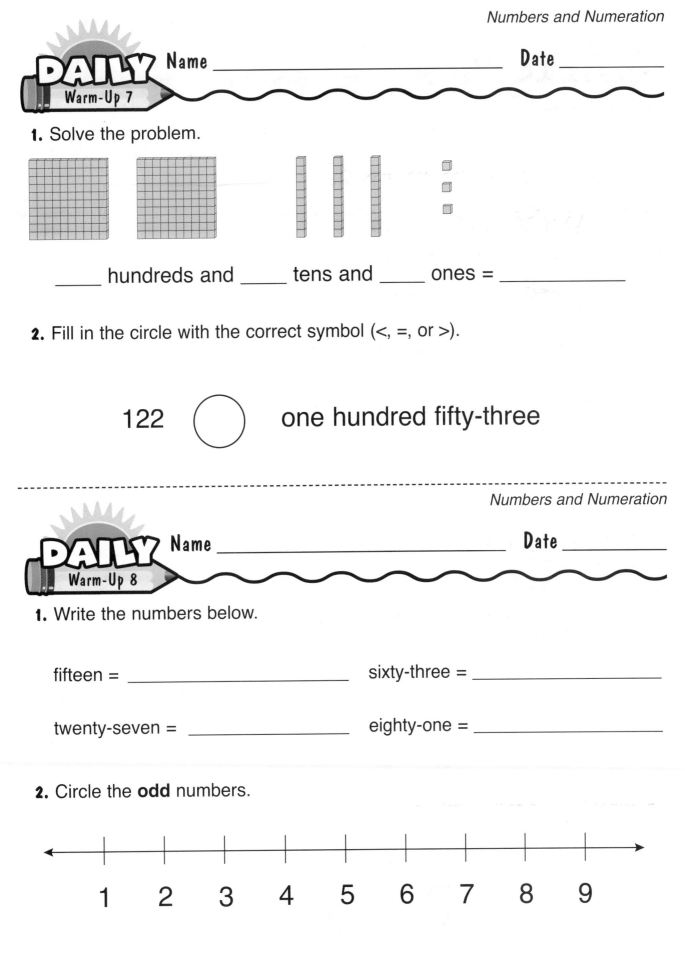

_____ hundreds and _____ tens and _____ ones = _____

2. Fill in the circle with the correct symbol (<, =, or >).

122 ◯ one hundred fifty-three

DAILY
Warm-Up 8

Name _____ Date _____

1. Write the numbers below.

fifteen = _____   sixty-three = _____

twenty-seven = _____   eighty-one = _____

2. Circle the **odd** numbers.

1   2   3   4   5   6   7   8   9

DAILY Warm-Up 9 | **Name** _____ **Date** _____

1. Three friends have numbers printed on their shirts. If they try to line up side-by-side to make a number, what is the largest number they could make? (*Write the answer on the line.*)

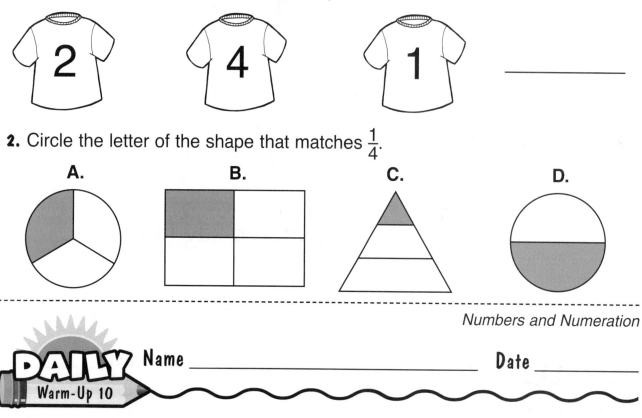

2   4   1   _____

2. Circle the letter of the shape that matches $\frac{1}{4}$.

   A.   **B.**   **C.**   **D.**

DAILY Warm-Up 10 | **Name** _____ **Date** _____

1. In the number 135, which digit is in the **ones** place? (*Circle the correct letter.*)

   A. one   **C.** three

   B. five   **D.** zero

2. Circle the number that is closest to 712.

   710   720   750

Name _____ Date _____

Warm-Up 11

1. Make tally marks to show 23.

2. Fill in the oval with the correct symbol (<, =, or >).

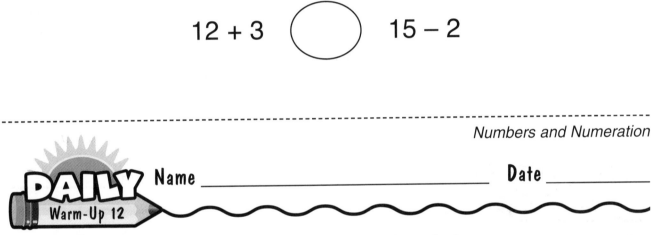

$$12 + 3 \quad \bigcirc \quad 15 - 2$$

Name _____ Date _____

Warm-Up 12

1. Write a number that is between the two numbers below.

375, _____, 377

2. Write the fractions.

A.

B.

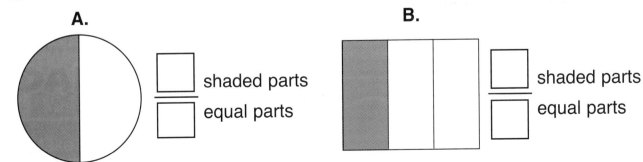

shaded parts

equal parts

shaded parts

equal parts

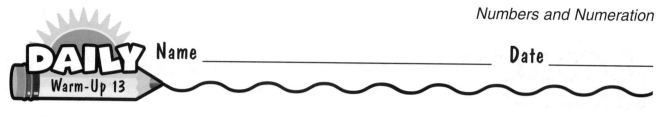

DAILY Warm-Up 13

Name _____ Date _____

1. Answer the problem below.

5 tens + 6 ones = _____

2. The table shows how many points three friends earned playing a video game. Which group shows these points in order from the largest to the smallest? (*Circle the correct letter.*)

A.	67	38	45
B.	38	45	67
C.	67	45	38
D.	38	67	45

Friends	Sam	Pam	Pete
Points Earned	45	67	38

DAILY Warm-Up 14

Name _____ Date _____

1. Jim had 18 baseball cards. Sam has 14 baseball cards and Hank has 9 baseball cards. Lee has the most cards. He has 23. How many baseball cards do Lee and Jim have combined? (*Record your answer on the grid.*)

Tens	Ones
①	①
②	②
③	③
④	④
⑤	⑤
⑥	⑥
⑦	⑦
⑧	⑧
⑨	⑨

2. Circle the letter of the fraction the model below represents.

A. $\frac{1}{3}$

B. $\frac{1}{4}$

C. $\frac{1}{2}$

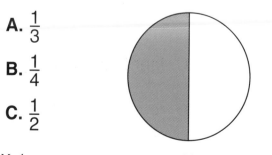

DAILY Warm-Up 15

Name _____ Date _____

1. Robin bought two bags of oranges. Altogether she has 139 oranges. Her family ate 12 oranges. How do you write the number of oranges she has left? (*Circle the correct letter.*)

   A. one hundred thirty-nine

   B. one hundred twenty

   C. one hundred seven

   D. one hundred twenty-seven

2. What numbers are missing? (*Write the numbers in the boxes.*)

10	20	30			60

DAILY Warm-Up 16

Name _____ Date _____

1. Seth wrote the numbers 1, 6, and 9 on separate cards. Seth laid the cards side-by-side to make different numbers. Circle the letter of the largest number Seth made with the cards.

   A. 9 1 6   **C.** 1 6 9

   B. 1 9 6   **D.** 9 6 1

2. Sandy counted 436 apples on a tree. How do you write the number of apples she counted? (*Circle the correct letter.*)

   A. four hundred sixty-three   **C.** four hundred thirty-six

   B. four thirty-six   **D.** four hundred three

Name _____

Date _____

1. What is the place value of the 6 in the number 693? (*Circle the correct letter.*)

A. hundreds   **B.** tens   **C.** ones

2. What is the place value of each of the underlined numbers? (*Write the answers on the lines.*)

A.	**B.**	**C.**
2<u>8</u>5	28<u>5</u>	<u>2</u>85
_____	_____	_____

- -

Name _____

Date _____

1. Solve the problems.

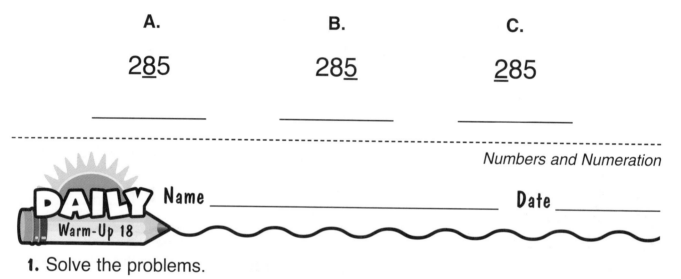

	Tens	Ones
84 =		
12 =		
53 =		

2. 2, 4, 6, 8, and 9 are even numbers. (*Circle the correct answer.*)

True   False

DAILY Warm-Up 19

Name _____ Date _____

1. Write the number of each of the following problems on the lines below.

twenty-seven	eighty	fourteen	one hundred five
_____	_____	_____	_____
forty-four	ninety-seven	forty	one hundred sixty
_____	_____	_____	_____

2. Write how many hundreds, tens, and ones are shown.

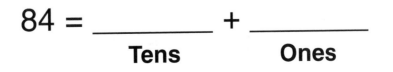

_____ _____ _____ _____
Hundreds   **Tens**   **Ones**

DAILY Warm-Up 20

Name _____ Date _____

1. On the lines, write the numbers below in words.

27 _____

145 _____

89 _____

46 _____

2. Write the number of tens and ones in the number 84.

$$84 = \underline{\hspace{2cm}} + \underline{\hspace{2cm}}$$
Tens   **Ones**

DAILY
Warm-Up 21

Name _____ Date _____

1. Circle the fraction that names the shaded part.

$\frac{1}{5}$　　　$\frac{3}{5}$　　　$\frac{2}{5}$

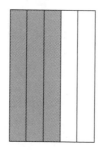

2. Brandi has 45¢. Maci has 8¢ more than Brandi. How much money does Maci have? (*Write your answer on the line.*)

+ ＿＿＿＿ = _____ ¢

- -

DAILY
Warm-Up 22

Name _____ Date _____

1. George's mother gave him some money. Write how much money George has on the line.

= _____ ¢

2. Peter picked 148 apples off an apple tree. On the line, write the number 148 in words.

_____

DAILY Warm-Up 23

Name _____ Date _____

1. Complete the charts by putting an **X** in the correct box. The first one is done for you.

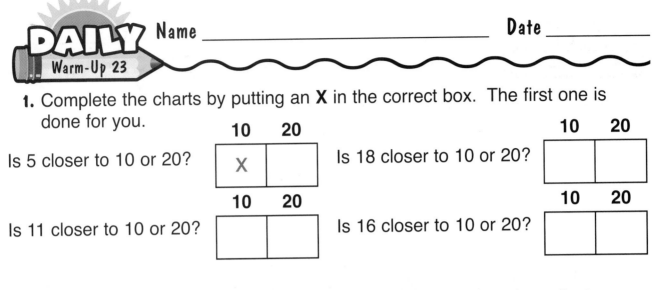

Is 5 closer to 10 or 20?

10	20
X	

Is 18 closer to 10 or 20?

10	20

Is 11 closer to 10 or 20?

10	20

Is 16 closer to 10 or 20?

10	20

2. Look at the list of numbers below. What are the largest and smallest numbers in the list? (*Write your answers on the line.*)

87, 84, 43, 98, 34

Smallest number: _____   Largest number: _____

DAILY Warm-Up 24

Name _____ Date _____

1. Look at the number line. What numbers are missing? (*Write your answers in the boxes.*)

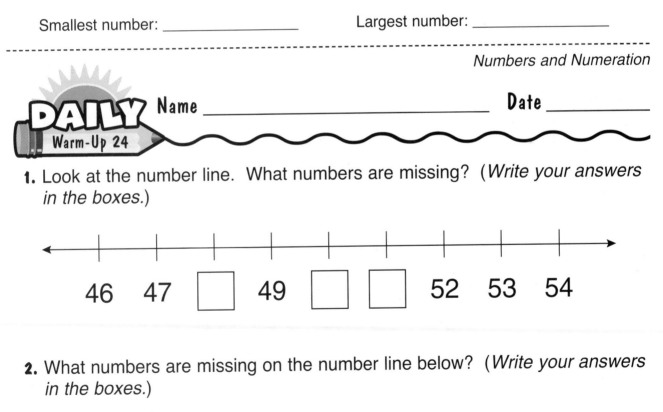

46   47   ☐   49   ☐   ☐   52   53   54

2. What numbers are missing on the number line below? (*Write your answers in the boxes.*)

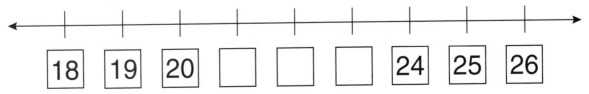

18 19 20 ☐ ☐ ☐ 24 25 26

DAILY Warm-Up 25

Name _____ Date _____

1. What number is one less than 423? (*Circle the correct letter.*)

A. 424   **B.** 422   **C.** 420

2. Which picture shows $\frac{1}{2}$ of the pie? (*Circle the correct letter.*)

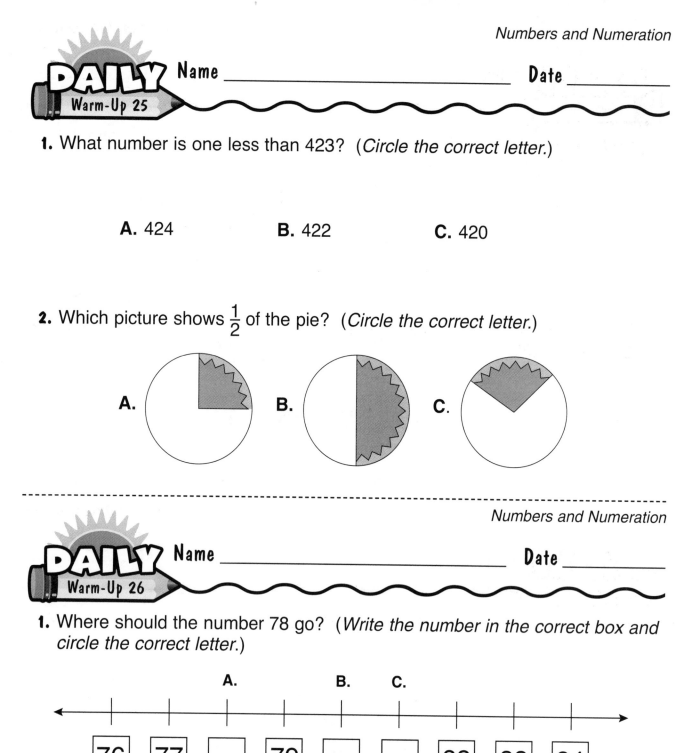

A.   **B.**   **C.**

DAILY Warm-Up 26

Name _____ Date _____

1. Where should the number 78 go? (*Write the number in the correct box and circle the correct letter.*)

A.   B.   C.

| 76 | 77 | | 79 | | | 82 | 83 | 84 |

2. What number is one more than 110? (*Circle the correct letter.*)

A. one hundred ten   **C.** one hundred nine

B. one hundred eleven   **D.** one hundred twelve

Name _____   **Date** _____

1. Which object below costs the most? (*Circle the correct letter.*)

A.

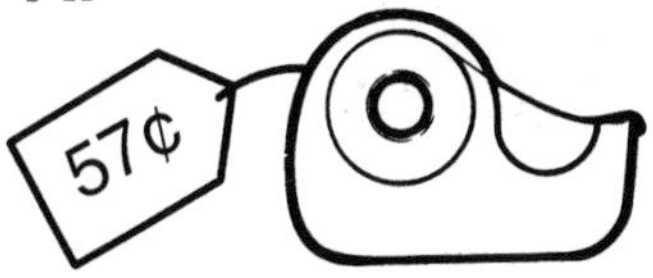

B.

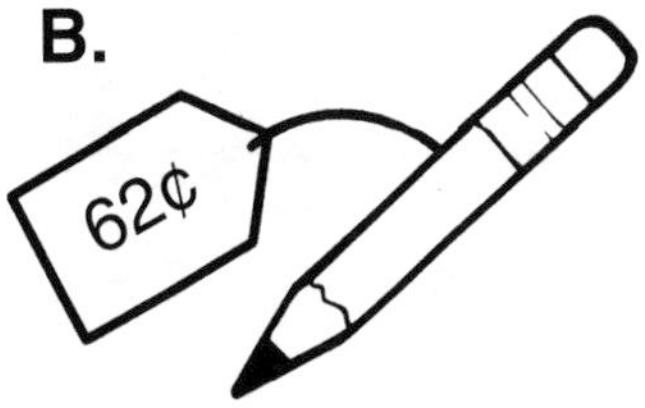

57¢   62¢

2. Which number has a 3 in the ones place and a 9 in the tens place? (*Circle the correct letter.*)

A. 392   **B.** 439   **C.** 593   **D.** 239

Name _____   **Date** _____

1. Which symbol belongs in the oval? (*Circle the correct letter.*)

15 ⬭ 7 + 8

A. >   **B.** <   **C.** =

2. How is the number 97 written? (*Circle the correct letter.*)

A. nine seven   **C.** seventy-nine

B. ninety-seven   **D.** nine and seven

DAILY Warm-Up 29   Name _____   Date _____

1. What fraction of the circles have the number 2 printed on them? (*Circle the correct letter.*)

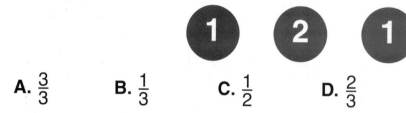

A. $\frac{3}{3}$ **B.** $\frac{1}{3}$ **C.** $\frac{1}{2}$ **D.** $\frac{2}{3}$

2. Which number is missing from the number line? (*Circle the correct letter.*)

A. 67

B. 68

C. 69

D. 70

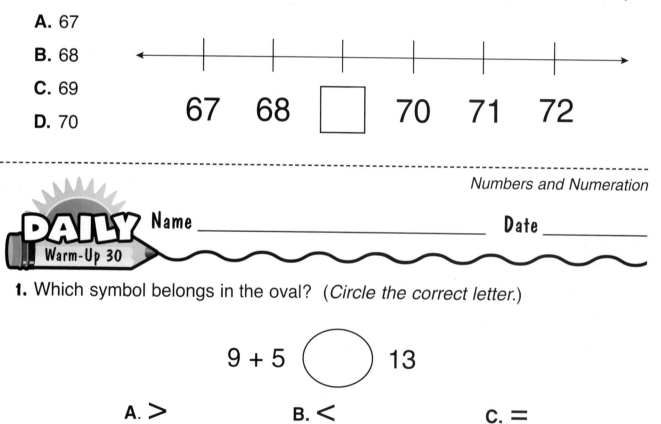

67   68   ☐   70   71   72

- -

DAILY Warm-Up 30   Name _____   Date _____

1. Which symbol belongs in the oval? (*Circle the correct letter.*)

$$9 + 5 \;\bigcirc\; 13$$

A. $>$ **B.** $<$ **C.** $=$

2. Which rectangle shows $\frac{3}{4}$ shaded? (*Circle the correct letter.*)

A.   **B.**   **C.**

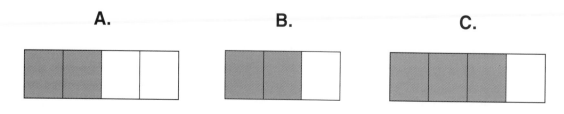

DAILY Warm-Up 31

Name _____ Date _____

1. Circle the pumpkin with the largest number.

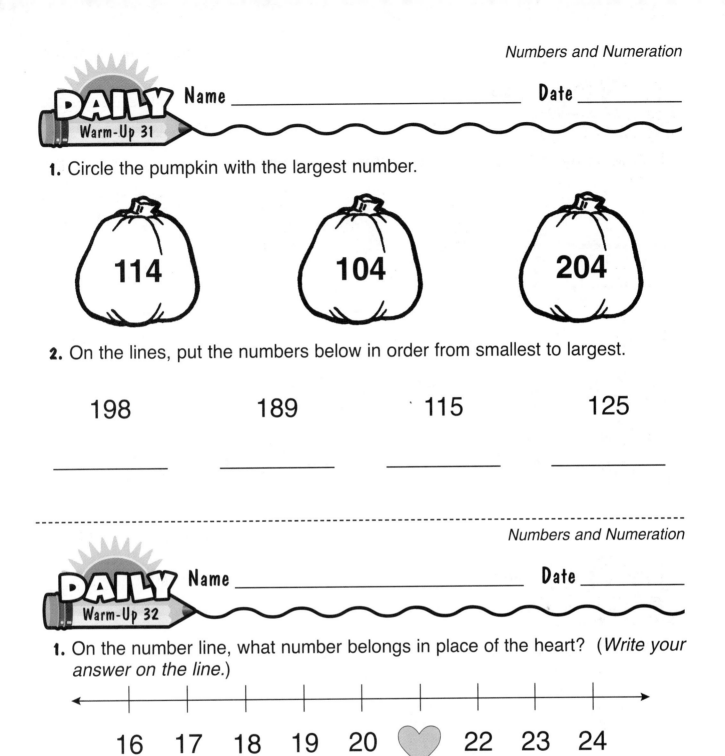

114   104   204

2. On the lines, put the numbers below in order from smallest to largest.

198   189   115   125

_____   _____   _____   _____

DAILY Warm-Up 32

Name _____ Date _____

1. On the number line, what number belongs in place of the heart? (*Write your answer on the line.*)

16   17   18   19   20   ♥   22   23   24

♥ = _____

2. Write the numbers that come between 43 and 49.

43, _____, _____, _____, _____, _____, 49

Name _____ **Date** _____

1. How many are shaded below? (*Write in your answer in the chart.*)

Hundreds	Tens	Ones

2. Who has the **most** money? _____

Hank

_____ ¢

Gale

_____ ¢

Name _____ **Date** _____

1. Which answer shows **forty-nine**? (*Circle the correct letter.*)

A.

B.

C.

D.

2. What fraction of the rectangle is shaded? (*Write the correct answer.*)

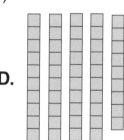

Name _____   **Date** _____

1. Nina found some money. How much money did Nina find? (*Write your answer on the line.*)

_____ ¢

2. How many parts of the rectangle are shaded? (*Write the top number of the fraction.*)

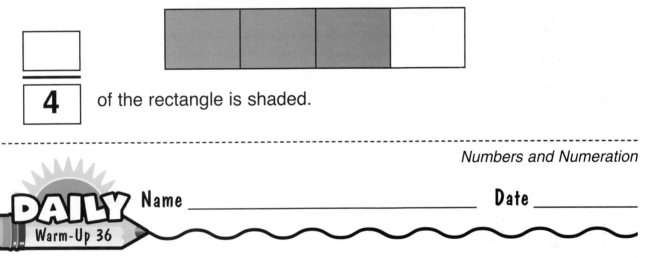

☐
4

of the rectangle is shaded.

Name _____   **Date** _____

1. What number is missing on the number line? (*Write your answer in the box.*)

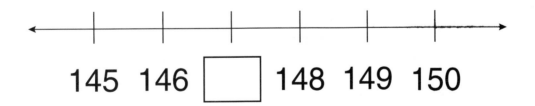

145 146 ☐ 148 149 150

2. Jerry picked 152 peaches from his grandfather's peach tree. How is this number written? (*Circle the correct letter.*)

A. one hundred twenty-five   **C.** one hundred five

B. one hundred fifty   **D.** one hundred fifty-two

DAILY Warm-Up 37

Name _____ Date _____

1. Circle the letter of the value of the underlined digit.

<u>2</u>37

A. ones   **B**. tens   **C**. hundreds

2. How many parts of the rectangle are shaded? (*Write the top number of the fraction.*)

[ ] / [4] of the rectangle is shaded.

- -

DAILY Warm-Up 38

Name _____ Date _____

1. What number is missing on the number line? (*Write your answer in the box.*)

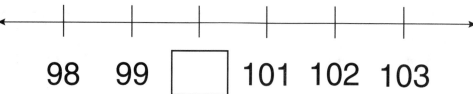

98   99   [ ]   101   102   103

2. There were 169 people at the movie theater. How is that number written? (*Circle the correct letter.*)

A. one hundred nine   **C**. one sixty nine

B. one hundred sixty   **D**. one hundred sixty-nine

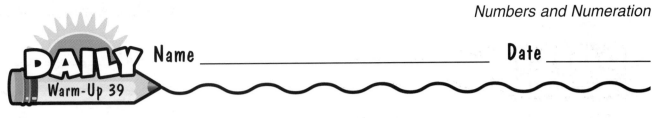

DAILY Warm-Up 39 Name _____ Date _____

1. Answer the problem below.

8 tens + 9 ones = _____

2. Write the number of points Pam scored in words.

Friends	Sam	Pam	Pete
Points Earned	45	67	38

Pam scored _____ points.

DAILY Warm-Up 40 Name _____ Date _____

1. Jake bought ninety-four balloons for a party. Fill in this number on the grid.

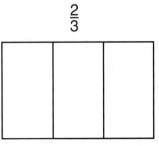

2. Shade in with your pencil the fractions below. (*The first one is done for you.*)

$\frac{1}{4}$ $\frac{1}{2}$ $\frac{2}{3}$

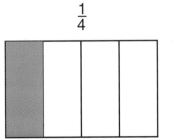
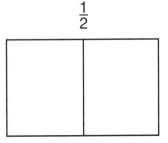

DAILY
Warm-Up 41

Name _____ Date _____

1. Circle *True* or *False*.

This coin is called a quarter. 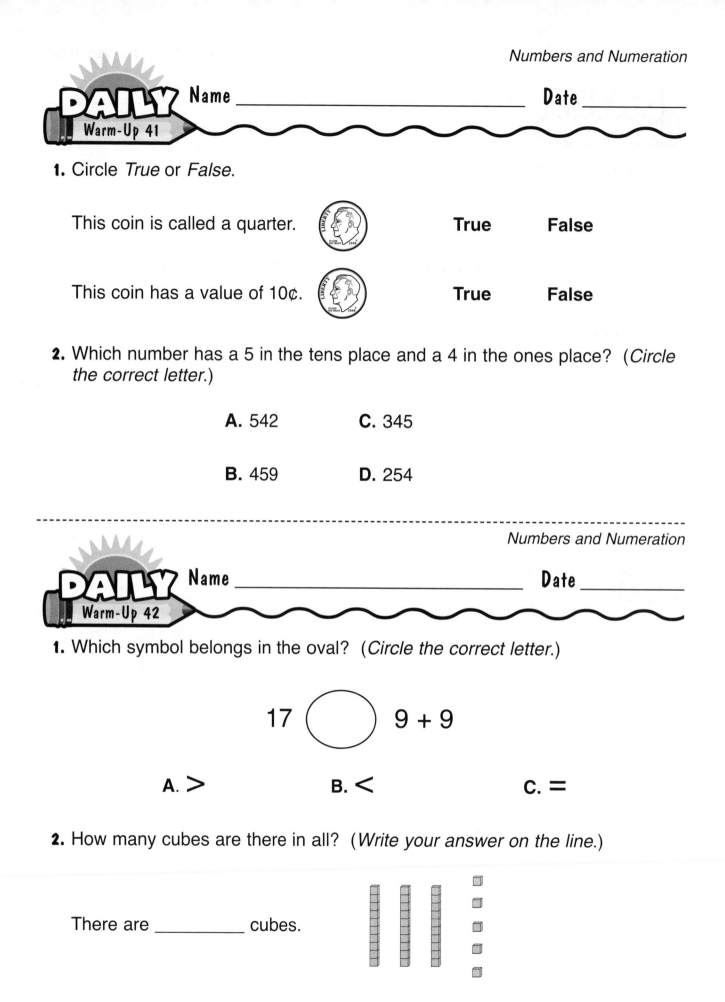   **True**   **False**

This coin has a value of 10¢.   **True**   **False**

2. Which number has a 5 in the tens place and a 4 in the ones place? (*Circle the correct letter.*)

A. 542   **C.** 345

B. 459   **D.** 254

DAILY
Warm-Up 42

Name _____ Date _____

1. Which symbol belongs in the oval? (*Circle the correct letter.*)

17 ◯ 9 + 9

A. >   **B.** <   **C.** =

2. How many cubes are there in all? (*Write your answer on the line.*)

There are _____ cubes.

DAILY Warm-Up 43

Name _____ Date _____

1. Solve the problem.

253 = _____ _____ _____

Hundreds   **Tens**   **Ones**

2. Circle the **sixth** letter below.

G   J   C   P   Y   L

DAILY Warm-Up 44

Name _____ Date _____

1. Write the number word for each numeral.

8 = _____   3 = _____

5 = _____   7 = _____

2. How many cubes are there in all? (*Write your answer on the line.*)

There are _____ cubes.

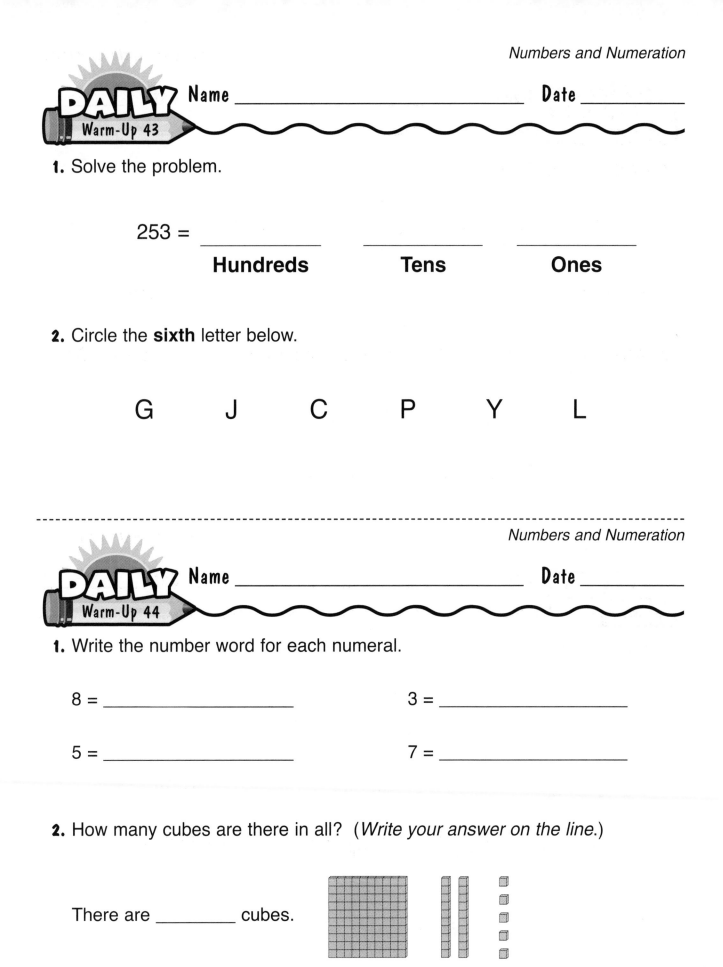

DAILY
Warm-Up 45

Name _____ Date _____

1. Solve the problem.

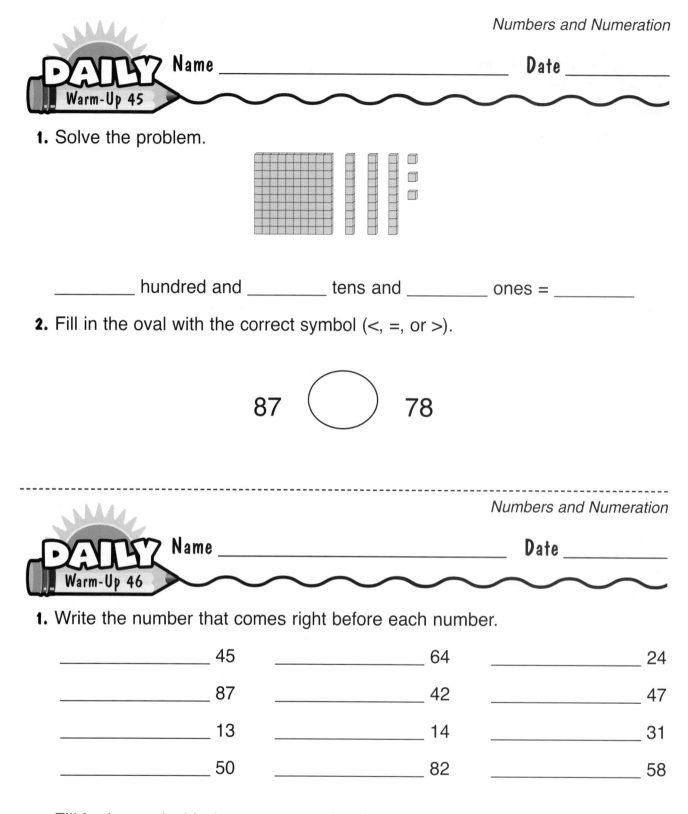

_____ hundred and _____ tens and _____ ones = _____

2. Fill in the oval with the correct symbol (<, =, or >).

87 ◯ 78

- -

DAILY
Warm-Up 46

Name _____ Date _____

1. Write the number that comes right before each number.

_____ 45	_____ 64	_____ 24
_____ 87	_____ 42	_____ 47
_____ 13	_____ 14	_____ 31
_____ 50	_____ 82	_____ 58

2. Fill in the oval with the correct symbol (<, =, or >).

4 + 6 ◯ 12 − 2

DAILY *Warm-Up 47*

Name _____   Date _____

1. Circle the digit in the hundreds place.

4 9 2

2. Circle the number below that has an 8 in the tens place.

8 2 4   **4 8 3**   **2 3 8**

DAILY *Warm-Up 48*

Name _____   Date _____

1. Becky wrote the numbers below. She asked her friend to write the missing numbers. What numbers did Becky's friend write? (*Fill in the answers.*)

165, _____, _____, 168

2. Write the fractions.

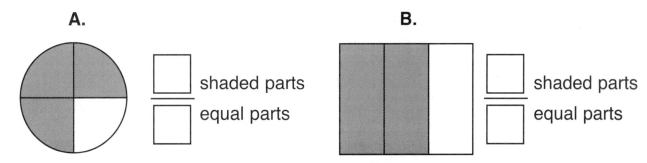

A.
⬚ shaded parts
⬚ equal parts

B.
⬚ shaded parts
⬚ equal parts

DAILY Warm-Up 49

Name _____ Date _____

1. Write the missing numbers in the boxes.

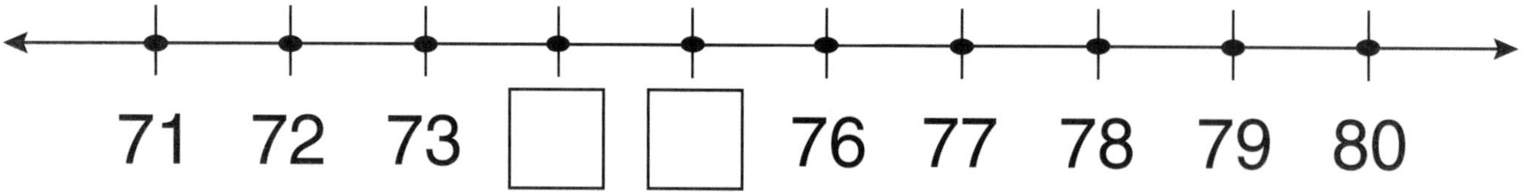

71   72   73   ☐   ☐   76   77   78   79   80

2. How much is shown below? (*Write your answers on the lines.*)

_____ tens and _____ ones = _____

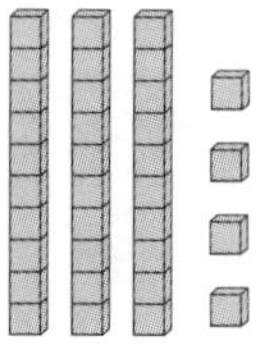

DAILY Warm-Up 50

Name _____ Date _____

1. What is the number for **five hundred sixty-three**? (*Circle the correct letter.*)

A. 506   **C.** 563

B. 560   **D.** 503

2. Write the fractions.

A.

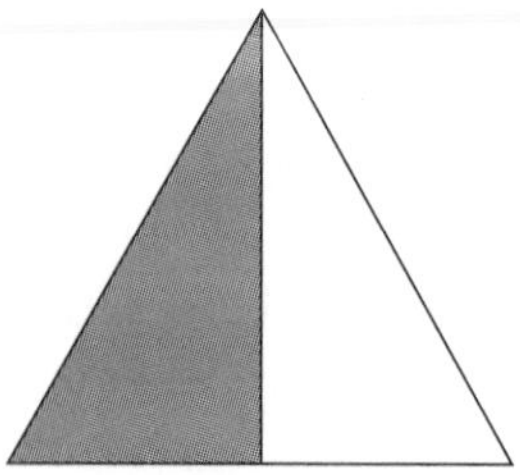

☐
—— shaded parts
☐ equal parts

B.

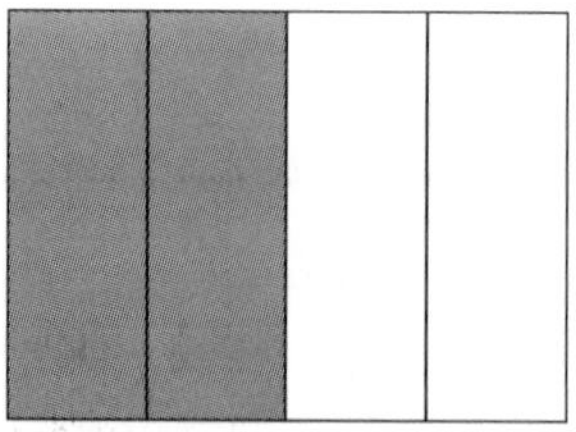

☐
—— shaded parts
☐ equal parts

DAILY Warm-Up 51

Name _____ Date _____

1. Circle the **seventh** bat.

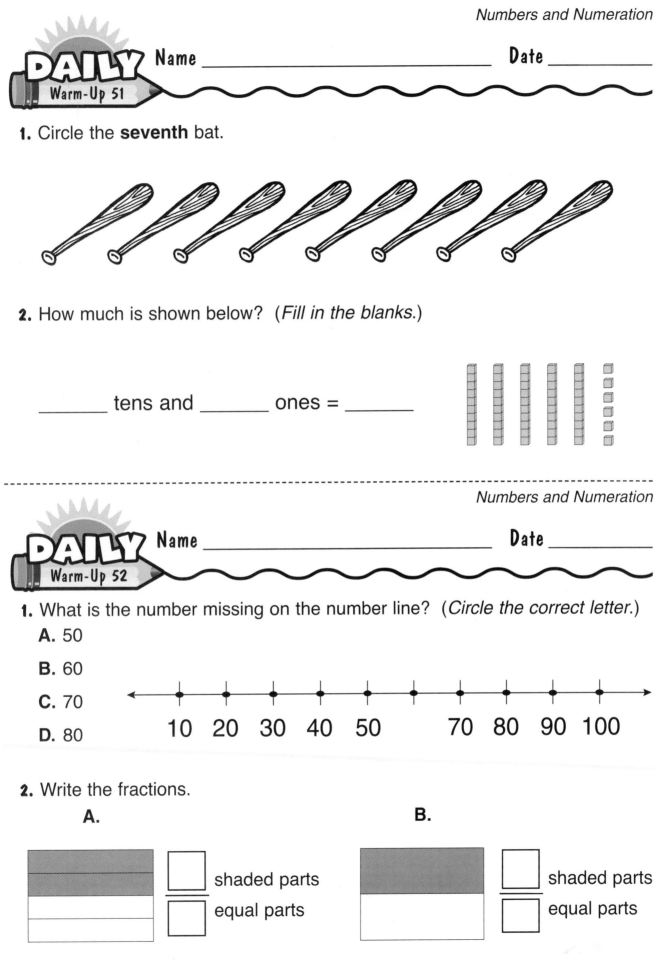

2. How much is shown below? (*Fill in the blanks.*)

_____ tens and _____ ones = _____

DAILY Warm-Up 52

Name _____ Date _____

1. What is the number missing on the number line? (*Circle the correct letter.*)

A. 50

B. 60

C. 70

D. 80

10   20   30   40   50   70   80   90   100

2. Write the fractions.

A.

_____ shaded parts
_____ equal parts

B.

_____ shaded parts
_____ equal parts

DAILY Warm-Up 53

Name _____ Date _____

1. Write these numbers in order from smallest to largest.

45   20   40   30   15

_____ _____ _____ _____ _____

2. Fill in the oval with the correct symbol (<, =, or >).

7 + 9 ◯ 20 − 4

DAILY Warm-Up 54

Name _____ Date _____

1. Circle the letter where the number 65 should go on the number line.

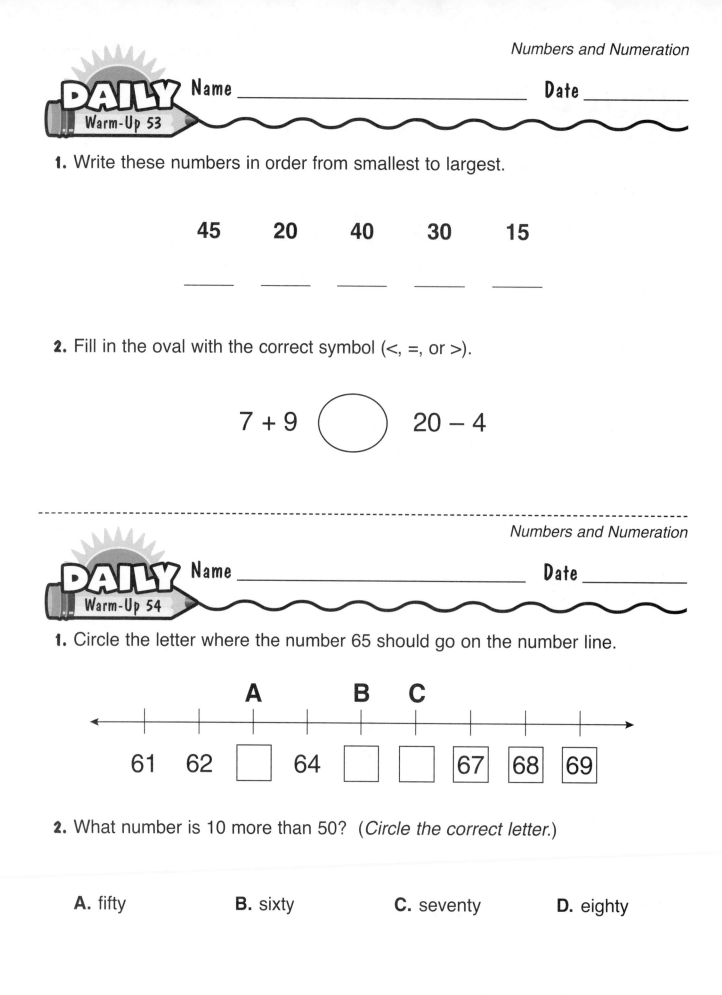

61   62   ☐   64   ☐   ☐   67   68   69

2. What number is 10 more than 50? (*Circle the correct letter.*)

A. fifty   **B.** sixty   **C.** seventy   **D.** eighty

DAILY Warm-Up 55

Name _____ Date _____

1. Brandi has 18¢. Maci has 9¢ less than Brandi. How much money does Maci have? (*Fill in your answer on the line.*)

Maci has _____ ¢

2. Which answer is **false**? (*Circle the correct letter.*)

A. 65 ⊘ sixty-three   **B.** 53 ⊜ fifty-nine   **C.** 42 ⊘ forty-seven

DAILY Warm-Up 56

Name _____ Date _____

1. Greg bought one dozen donuts. How many donuts are in one dozen? (*Fill in your answer on the line.*)

There are _____ donuts in one dozen.

2. In the number 592, which digit is in the tens place? (*Circle the correct letter.*)

A. 2   **B.** 9   **C.** 5

DAILY Name _____ Date _____
Warm-Up 57

1. What number is one more than 423? *(Circle the correct letter.)*

A. 424   **B.** 422   **C.** 420

2. Is the rectangle divided into four equal parts? *(Circle "Yes" or "No.")*

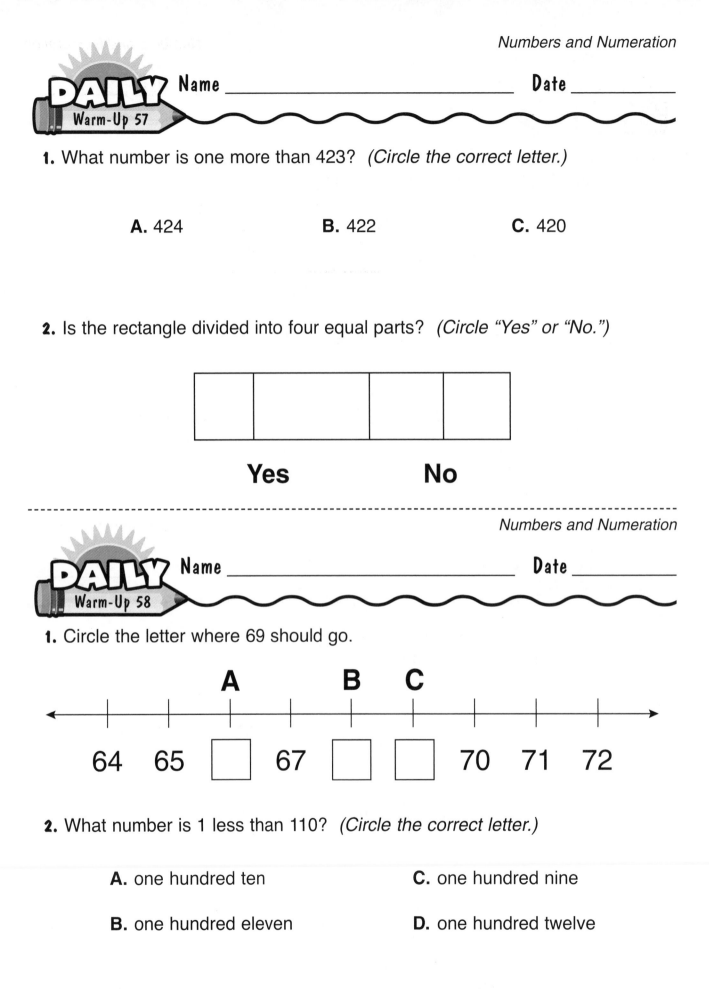

Yes   **No**

DAILY Name _____ Date _____
Warm-Up 58

1. Circle the letter where 69 should go.

A   B   C

64   65   ☐   67   ☐   ☐   70   71   72

2. What number is 1 less than 110? *(Circle the correct letter.)*

A. one hundred ten   **C.** one hundred nine

B. one hundred eleven   **D.** one hundred twelve

DAILY Warm-Up 59

Name _____ Date _____

1. Complete the chart by counting by tens.

10	20			50		70
80	90	100	110		130	140
150		170	180	190		210

2. Write the number for two hundred ninety-three on the line.

293

DAILY Warm-Up 60

Name _____ Date _____

1. Which number is one hundred thirty-eight? (*Circle the correct letter.*)

A. 283 **B.** 183 **C.** 138

2. Write these numbers in order from *largest to smallest*.

145	87	42	198	144	112

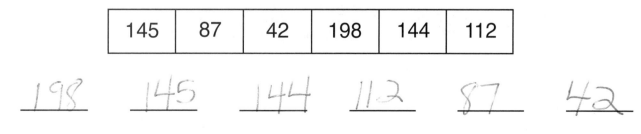

198   145   144   112   87   42

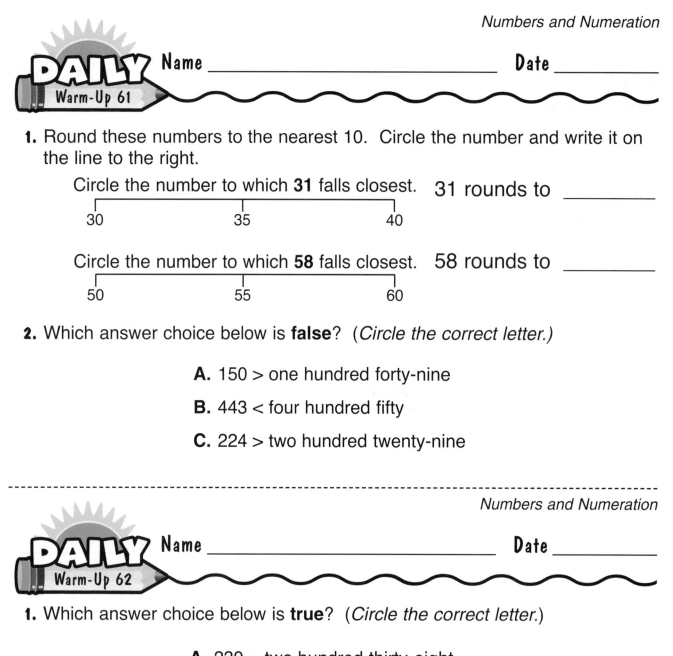

DAILY **Warm-Up 61**

Name _____   Date _____

1. Round these numbers to the nearest 10. Circle the number and write it on the line to the right.

Circle the number to which **31** falls closest.   31 rounds to _____

30   35   40

Circle the number to which **58** falls closest.   58 rounds to _____

50   55   60

2. Which answer choice below is **false**? (*Circle the correct letter.*)

    A. 150 > one hundred forty-nine

    B. 443 < four hundred fifty

    C. 224 > two hundred twenty-nine

DAILY **Warm-Up 62**

Name _____   Date _____

1. Which answer choice below is **true**? (*Circle the correct letter.*)

    A. 239 = two hundred thirty-eight

    B. 223 = two hundred twenty-three

    C. 410 = four hundred twenty

2. Jack has 7 stacks of pennies. Each stack has 10 pennies. How many total pennies does Jack have? (*Write the number in the boxes below.*)

Hundreds	Tens	Ones

Warm-Up 1
1. C
2.

Warm-Up 2
1. one hundred forty-eight
2. one hundred ninety-eight

Warm-Up 3
1. 8 x 4 = 32 or 4 x 8 = 32
2. D

Warm-Up 4
1. B
2.

Hundreds	Tens	Ones
	$8	7

Warm-Up 5
1.

Hundreds	Tens	Ones
	3	2

2. B

Warm-Up 6
1. D
2. 1/2 or one-half

Warm-Up 7
1. <u>2</u> hundreds and <u>3</u> tens and
   <u>3</u> ones = <u>233</u>
2. <

Warm-Up 8
1. 15, 27, 63, 81
2. 1, 3, 5, 7, 9

Warm-Up 9
1. 421
2. B

Warm-Up 10
1. B
2. 710

Warm-Up 11
1. 𝍶𝍶 𝍶𝍶 𝍶𝍶 𝍶𝍶 |||
2. >

Warm-Up 12
1. 376
2A. 1/2
2B. 1/3

Warm-Up 13
1. 56
2. C

Warm-Up 14
1. 41
2. C

Warm-Up 15
1. D
2. 40, 50

Warm-Up 16
1. D
2. C

Warm-Up 17
1. A
2A. tens
2B. ones
2C. hundreds

Warm-Up 18
1.

	Tens	Ones
84 =	8	4
12 =	1	2
53 =	5	3

2. False

Warm-Up 19
1. 27, 80, 14, 105
   44, 97, 40, 160
2. 212

Warm-Up 20
1. twenty-seven, one hundred
   forty-five, eighty-nine,
   forty-six
2. 8 tens + 4 ones

Warm-Up 21
1. 3/5
2. 53¢

Warm-Up 22
1. 94¢
2. one hundred forty-eight

Warm-Up 23
1. 5 is closer to 10
   11 is closer to 10
   18 is closer to 20
   16 is closer to 20
2. Smallest: 34
   Largest: 98

Warm-Up 24
1. 48, 50, 51
2. 21, 22, 23

Warm-Up 25
1. B
2. B

Warm-Up 26
1. A
2. B

Warm-Up 27
1. B
2. C

Warm-Up 28
1. C
2. B

Warm-Up 29
1. B
2. C

Warm-Up 30
1. A
2. C

Warm-Up 31
1. 204
2. 115, 125, 189, 198

Warm-Up 32
1. 21
2. 44, 45, 46, 47, 48

Warm-Up 33
1.

Hundreds	Tens	Ones
1	4	5

2. Gale

Warm-Up 34
1. D
2. 1/4

Warm-Up 35
1. 62¢
2. 3

Warm-Up 36
1. 147
2. D

Warm-Up 37
1. C
2. 1

Warm-Up 38
1. 100
2. D

Warm-Up 39
1. 89
2. sixty-seven

Warm-Up 40
1. 94 (grid)
2. 1/2 shaded, 2/3 shaded

Warm-Up 41
1. False
   True
2. D

Warm-Up 42
1. B
2. 35

Warm-Up 43
1. 2 hundreds, 5 tens, 3 ones
2. L

Warm-Up 44
1. eight, five, three, seven
2. 125

Warm-Up 45
1. 1 hundred and 3 tens and 3 ones = 133
2. >

Warm-Up 46
1. 44, 86, 12, 49, 63, 41, 13, 81, 23, 46, 30, 57
2. =

Warm-Up 47
1. 4
2. 483

Warm-Up 48
1. 166, 167
2A. 3/4
2B. 2/3

Warm-Up 49
1. 74, 75
2. 3 tens and 4 ones = 34

Warm-Up 50
1. C
2A. 1/2
2B. 2/4

Warm-Up 51
1. Seventh bat should be circled.
2. 5 tens and 6 ones = 56

Warm-Up 52
1. B
2A. 2/4
2B. 1/2

Warm-Up 53
1. 15, 20, 30, 40, 45
2. =

Warm-Up 54
1. B
2. B

Warm-Up 55
1. 9¢
2. B

Warm-Up 56
1. 12
2. B

Warm-Up 57
1. A
2. No

Warm-Up 58
1. C
2. C

Warm-Up 59
1. 30, 40, 60, 120, 160, 200
2. 293

Warm-Up 60
1. C
2. 198, 145, 144, 112, 87, 42

Warm-Up 61
1. 30, 60
2. C

Warm-Up 62
1. B
2. 7 tens and 0 ones

OPERATIONS

DAILY
Warm-Up 1

Name _____ Date _____

1. Terry added 15 to a number and got the number displayed on the calculator. What number did she add to make 53? *(Write your answer on the line.)*

| 53 |

7	8	9	÷
4	5	6	x
1	2	3	−
0		=	+

| ON/C | CE | % |

_____

2. Mark is learning to play the guitar. He practiced 2 hours on Monday, 3 hours on Tuesday, and 4 hours on Wednesday. How many hours did Mark practice altogether? *(Write your answer on the line.)*

_____ hours

DAILY
Warm-Up 2

Name _____ Date _____

1. Jack has 12 yellow toy cars. His cousin gave him 5 more. Which model below shows how many toy cars Jack now has? *(Circle the correct letter.)*

A.   B.   C.   D.

2. Answer the problem below.

$$74 - \text{\underline{\hspace{1cm}}} = 17$$

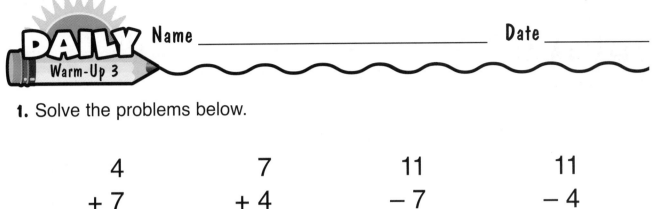

DAILY Warm-Up 3

Name _____ Date _____

1. Solve the problems below.

$$\begin{array}{r} 4 \\ +\,7 \\ \hline \end{array} \qquad \begin{array}{r} 7 \\ +\,4 \\ \hline \end{array} \qquad \begin{array}{r} 11 \\ -\,7 \\ \hline \end{array} \qquad \begin{array}{r} 11 \\ -\,4 \\ \hline \end{array}$$

2. Mary had 2 cubes, 3 triangles, and 6 rectangles. How many total shapes does Mary have? *(Write your answer on the line.)*

_____ shapes

DAILY Warm-Up 4

Name _____ Date _____

1. George bought 2 packages of crayons. There are 12 crayons in each package. How many crayons does George now have? *(Write your answer on the line.)*

_____ crayons

2. Jack and Ryan played basketball. Jack scored 32 points and Ryan scored 8 points. How many more points did Jack score than Ryan? *(Write your answer on the line.)*

_____ more points

DAILY Warm-Up 5

Name _____ Date _____

1. There are 248 students at Dawson Elementary. Seventy-eight students went on a field trip. How many students were left at school? *(Circle the correct letter.)*

A. 170

B. 326

C. 230

2. Fill in the circle with the correct symbol (<, >, or =).

174 ◯ 471

DAILY Warm-Up 6

Name _____ Date _____

1. Mark and Jim are playing cards. They make a mark by their name for each game they win. How many games did Mark win? *(Write your answer on the line.)*

Mark won _____ games.

Games Won	
Jim	Mark
ЖЖ ЖЖ ЖЖ ЖЖ III	ЖЖ ЖЖ II

2. Write the answer to the problem on the line.

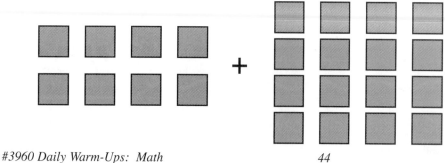 + 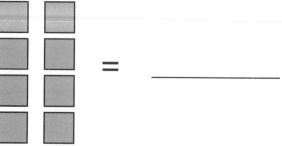 = _____

DAILY
Warm-Up 7

Name _____   Date _____

1. Solve the problem below.

$$17 + 3 = 20$$

so

$$20 - 3 = \boxed{}$$

2. Sandra baked 28 cupcakes. Beth baked 24 cupcakes. How many cupcakes did Sandra and Beth bake altogether? *(Write your answer on the line.)*

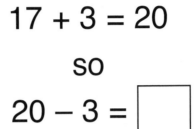

_____ cupcakes

DAILY
Warm-Up 8

Name _____   Date _____

1. Jerry has 8 blue shirts and 4 green shirts. His mother bought him 6 yellow shirts. How many shirts does Jerry have now? *(Write your answer on the line.)*

_____ shirts

2. Solve the problem.

$$2 \times 4 = \underline{}$$

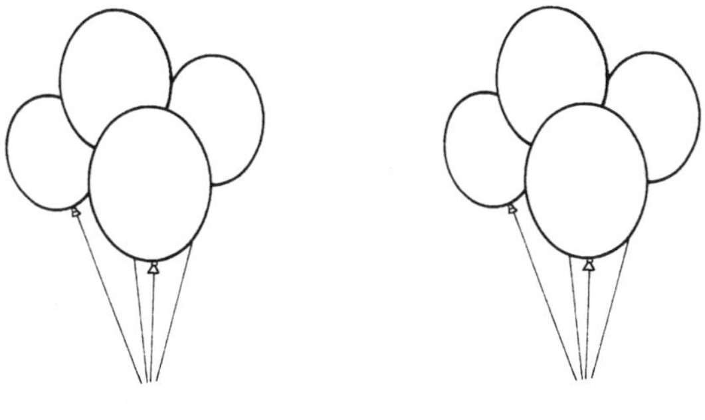

DAILY Warm-Up 9 — Name _____ Date _____

1. Use some of the numbers in the box to make a subtraction problem.

| 16 | 31 | 7 | 23 |

_____ − _____ = _____

2. Sue had 12 buttons on her dress. Four buttons fell off. How many buttons does Sue have left? *(Circle the correct answer letter.)*

A. 3 **B.** 8 **C.** 6

DAILY Warm-Up 10 — Name _____ Date _____

1. List sets of three numbers that add to 14. *(The first one is done for you.)*

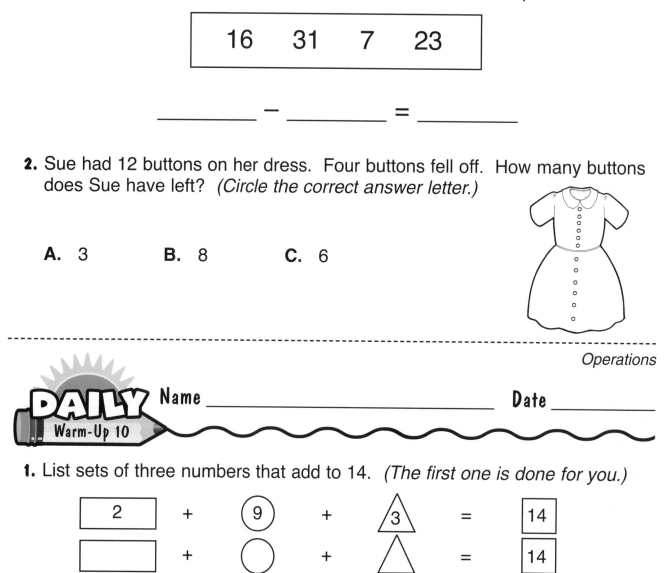

| 2 | + | 9 | + | 3 | = | 14 |

___ + ◯ + △ = 14

___ + ◯ + △ = 14

2. Mary has 16 blue ribbons. Jenny has 12 green ribbons and Marsha has 14 pink ribbons. How many ribbons do Mary and Marsha have together? *(Write your answer on the line.)*

_____ ribbons

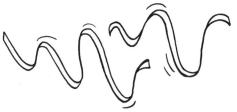

DAILY Warm-Up 11   Name _____   Date _____

1. Answer the problems below.

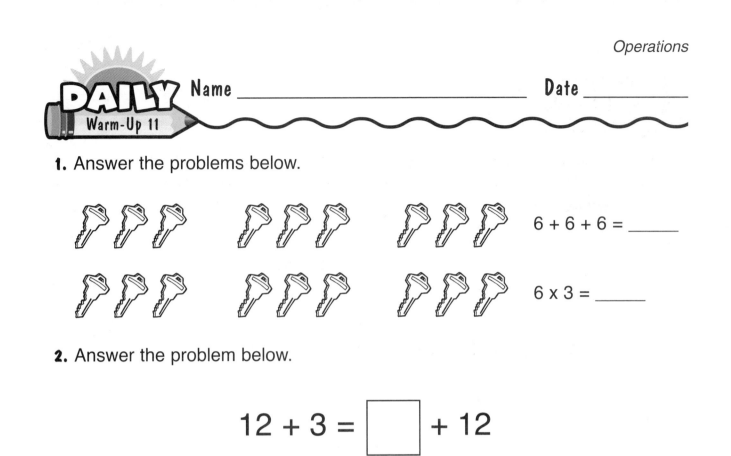

6 + 6 + 6 = _____

6 x 3 = _____

2. Answer the problem below.

$$12 + 3 = \boxed{} + 12$$

- -

DAILY Warm-Up 12   Name _____   Date _____

1. Answer the problems below.

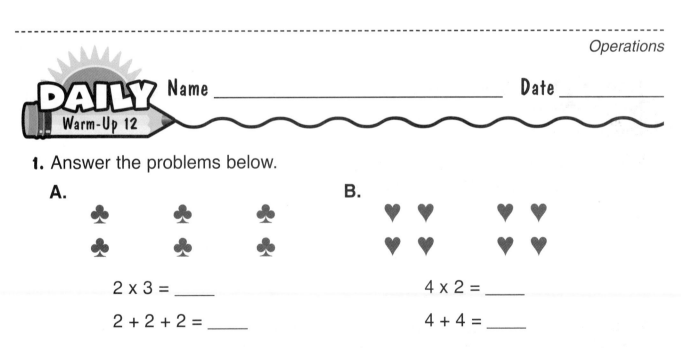

A.

2 x 3 = ____

2 + 2 + 2 = ____

B.

4 x 2 = ____

4 + 4 = ____

2. Nancy baked a dozen cookies. Her brother ate half of the cookies. How many cookies were left? *(Write your answer on the line.)*

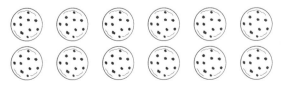

_____ cookies

Name _____ **Date** _____

DAILY Warm-Up 13

1. Isaac has 59 smile stickers. He put some smile stickers on his papers. He now has 32 smile stickers left. How many smile stickers did he use? *(Write your answer on the line.)*

_____ stickers

2. Write a word problem for the equation $(7 + 3 = 10)$.

_____

_____

_____

Name _____ **Date** _____

DAILY Warm-Up 14

1. Susan had 3 vases. Each vase had 2 flowers. How many flowers were there altogether? *(Write your answer on the line.)*

_____ flowers

2. Solve the subtraction problem.

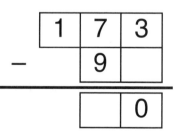

	1	7	3
−		9	
			0

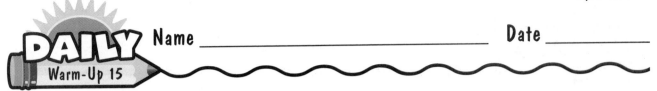

DAILY Warm-Up 15 **Name** ______________________ **Date** __________

1. Lee puts a dozen eggs on the stove. He put cheese on half the eggs. How many eggs do not have cheese? *(Write your answer on the line.)*

__________ eggs do not have cheese

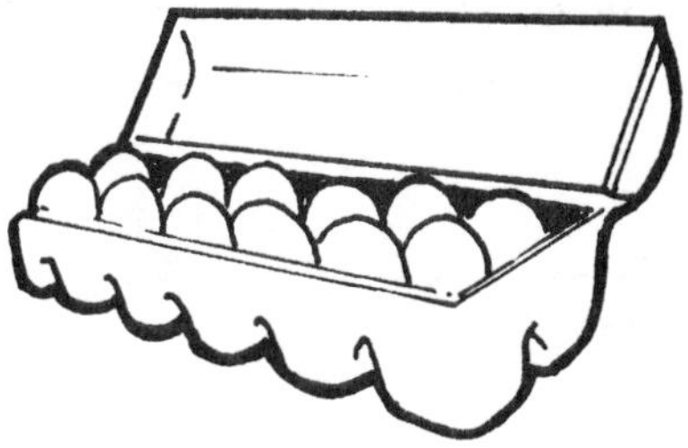

2. Answer the problem below.

$$4 + 5 - 3 = \underline{\qquad\qquad}$$

Operations

DAILY Warm-Up 16 **Name** ______________________ **Date** __________

1. Ty had 25 blocks. He got 8 more for his birthday. How many blocks does he now have? *(Circle the correct letter.)*

A. 17 **B.** 33 **C.** 23

2. What number is five more than 14 – 6? *(Circle the correct letter.)*

A. 8 **B.** 13 **C.** 14

DAILY Warm-Up 17 Name _____ Date _____

1. Ty scored 34 points playing basketball. Cody scored 46 points. How many more points did Cody score than Ty? *(Write the math problem on the line and solve.)*

_____

2. Mr. Todd is planning an art project for his class. He puts 3 paintbrushes in each of the 5 containers the class will be using. How many paintbrushes are there in all? *(Write your answer on the line.)*

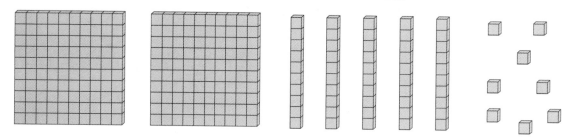

_____

- -

DAILY Warm-Up 18 Name _____ Date _____

1. How many blocks are shown below? _____

2. Solve the problem. *(Circle the correct letter.)*

A. 2

B. 3

C. 6 $6 \div 2 =$ _____

D. 8

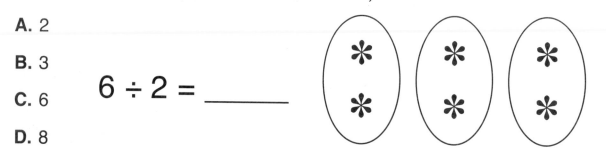

Name _____ **Date** _____

Warm-Up 19

1. Maci read thirteen books last week. She read fifteen books this week. How many books has Maci read? *(Circle the correct letter.)*

    A. 13   **B.** 25   **C.** 28

2. The scoreboard shows the final score from the game the Dawson Elementary teachers played for their students. By how many points did the 4th grade win? *(Write your answer on the line.)*

_____ points

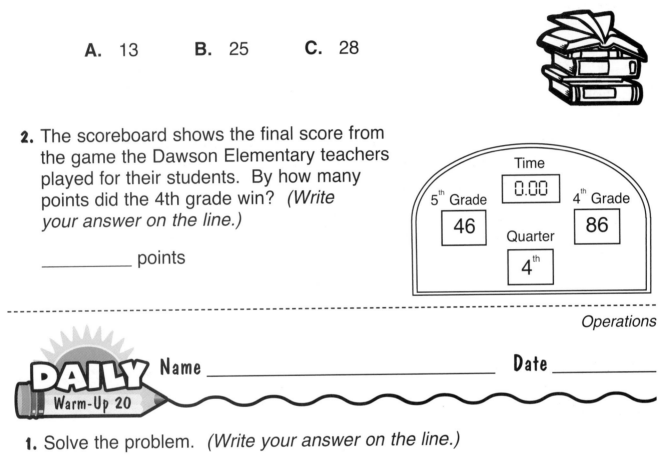

Time
0.00

5th Grade   4th Grade

46   86

Quarter

4th

- -

Name _____ **Date** _____

Warm-Up 20

1. Solve the problem. *(Write your answer on the line.)*

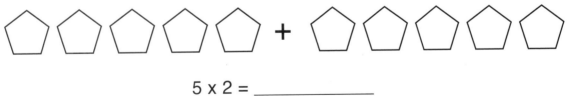

$$5 \times 2 = \underline{\hspace{2cm}}$$

2. Jason has 34 football cards. For his birthday, his mother gave him 9 more. How many cards does Jason have in total?

Explain how to get the answer: _____

_____

_____

_____

Name _____   **Date** _____

1. Solve the problem below. Use the symbol >, <, or =.

$$17 + 9 \bigcirc 19 + 4$$

2. Jackson picked 98 berries for his grandmother to use in her pie. On their way back to their grandmother's house, he and his sister ate 34 berries. How many berries does Jackson have left to give his grandmother? *(Write your answer on the line.)*

_____ berries

Name _____   **Date** _____

1. Solve the problem. *(Write your answer on the line.)*

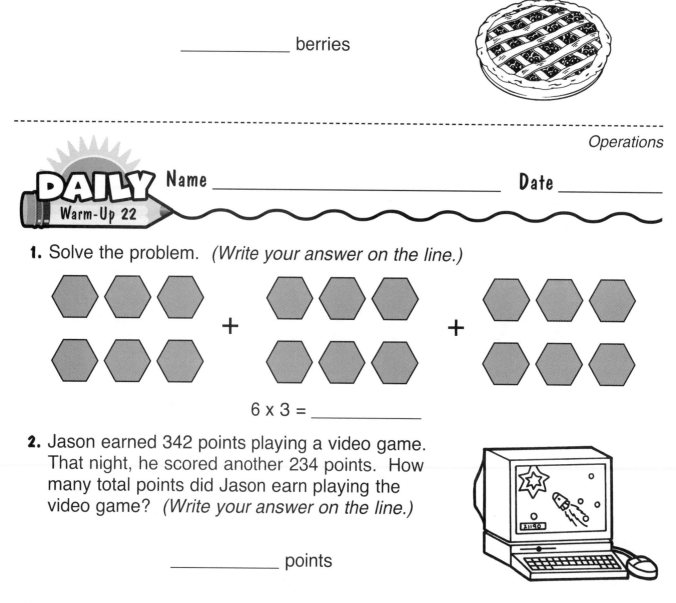

6 x 3 = _____

2. Jason earned 342 points playing a video game. That night, he scored another 234 points. How many total points did Jason earn playing the video game? *(Write your answer on the line.)*

_____ points

DAILY
Warm-Up 23

Name _____   Date _____

1. Six students in Mrs. Mann's class used the stapler three times during the day. How many times was the stapler used?

_____ times

2. Solve the problem below.

$$34 + 54 = \boxed{}$$

DAILY
Warm-Up 24

Name _____   Date _____

1. Diana invited 16 friends to her birthday party. Six friends did not come to the party. How many friends came to Diana's birthday party? *(Write your answer on the line.)*

_____ friends came to the party.

2. There are 2 socks to a pair. How many socks are in 8 pairs? *(Write your answer on the line.)*

_____ socks

DAILY Warm-Up 25

Name _____ Date _____

1. Meredith went to her uncle's farm. She saw 9 chickens, 4 cows, 3 pigs, and 7 horses. How many animals did she see in all? *(Write your answer on the line.)*

_____ animals

2. Solve the problems below.

$$3\,5$$
$$+\,4\,6$$

$$19 - 6 = \underline{\hspace{1cm}}$$

$$8\,4$$
$$+\,4\,3$$

$$34 - 9 = \underline{\hspace{1cm}}$$

- -

DAILY Warm-Up 26

Name _____ Date _____

1. Paul has four gray marbles. He found 6 more gray marbles under his bed. How many gray marbles does Paul now have? *(Circle the correct letter.)*

A. $6 + 4 = 10$

B. $6 - 4 = 2$

C. $10 = 4 = 6$

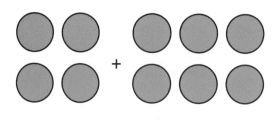

2. Jane had 30 stickers. She gave some stickers away. Now she has 15 stickers. How many stickers did Jane give away? *(Solve the problem and write your answer on the line.)*

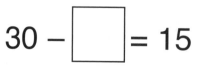

$$30 - \boxed{} = 15$$

She gave _____ stickers away.

DAILY Warm-Up 27

Name _____ Date _____

1. There are 98 seats on an airplane but only 56 passengers. How many seats are empty? *(Circle the correct letter.)*

   A. 38

   B. 42

   C. 154

2. Solve the problems below.

$$\begin{array}{r} 7\,3 \\ +\,7\,7 \\ \hline \end{array}$$ $49 - 3 =$ ____ $$\begin{array}{r} 6\,3 \\ +\,7\,8 \\ \hline \end{array}$$ $62 - 6 =$ ____

- -

DAILY Warm-Up 28

Name _____ Date _____

1. Mrs. Brown made 38 cupcakes. She gave 19 cupcakes to students. What operation should you use to find how many cupcakes were left? *(Circle the correct letter.)*

   A. 38 + 19 =

   B. 38 − 19 =

   C. 19 + 38 =

2. Solve the problem below.

$$24 - \boxed{} = 18$$

DAILY Warm-Up 29

Name _____ Date _____

1. There are 22 students in Mr. White's class. Some students leave and go to art class. There are now only 8 students left. How many students left for art class? *(Write your answer on the line.)*

_____ students left for art class.

2. Fill in the circle with the correct symbol. Use the symbols <, >, or =.

$$836 \bigcirc 863$$

DAILY Warm-Up 30

Name _____ Date _____

1. Sam and Fred played a game of basketball. They made a mark for each basket scored. How many more points did Fred score than Sam? *(Write your answer on the line.)*

_____ more points

Score Board	
Sam	Fred
⑷⑷	⑷⑷⑷

2. Solve the problem.

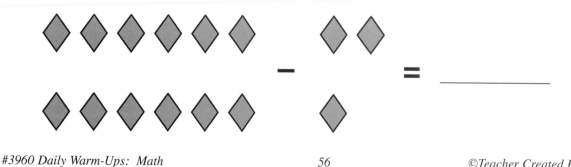

Name _____ **Date** _____

1. Which subtraction problem is done correctly? *(Circle the correct letter.)*

A.
```
  5 6
- 1 2
┌─┬─┐
│6│8│
└─┴─┘
```

B.
```
  5 6
- 1 5
┌─┬─┐
│7│1│
└─┴─┘
```

C.
```
  5 6
- 1 5
┌─┬─┐
│4│1│
└─┴─┘
```

D.
```
  6 6
- 4 5
┌─┬─┐
│1│1│
└─┴─┘
```

2. George has 16 horses and 12 cows. How many more horses than cows does George have? *(Write your answer on the line.)*

_____ more horses

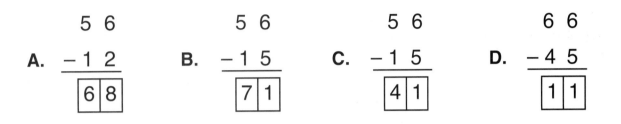

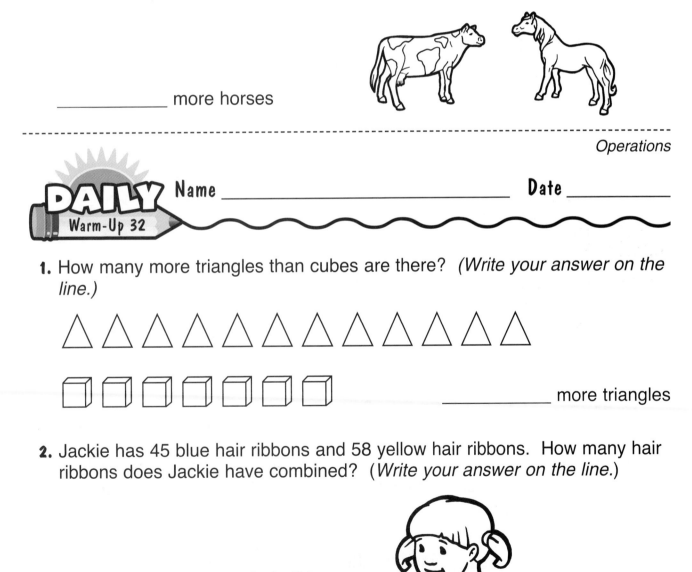

Name _____ **Date** _____

1. How many more triangles than cubes are there? *(Write your answer on the line.)*

_____ more triangles

2. Jackie has 45 blue hair ribbons and 58 yellow hair ribbons. How many hair ribbons does Jackie have combined? *(Write your answer on the line.)*

_____ hair ribbons

DAILY
Warm-Up 33

Name _____   **Date** _____

1. Which problem is **not** done correctly? *(Circle the correct letter.)*

A.
$$\begin{array}{r} 7\ 4 \\ -\ 1\ 2 \\ \hline \boxed{6}\ \boxed{2} \end{array}$$

B.
$$\begin{array}{r} 5\ 6 \\ -\ 2\ 5 \\ \hline \boxed{3}\ \boxed{1} \end{array}$$

C.
$$\begin{array}{r} 8\ 4 \\ -\ 2\ 2 \\ \hline \boxed{6}\ \boxed{2} \end{array}$$

D.
$$\begin{array}{r} 7\ 9 \\ -\ 2\ 6 \\ \hline \boxed{6}\ \boxed{3} \end{array}$$

2. Deron has 4 tractors. Each tractor has 4 wheels. How many wheels are there in all? *(Circle the correct letter.)*

A. 4   **B.** 8   **C.** 16

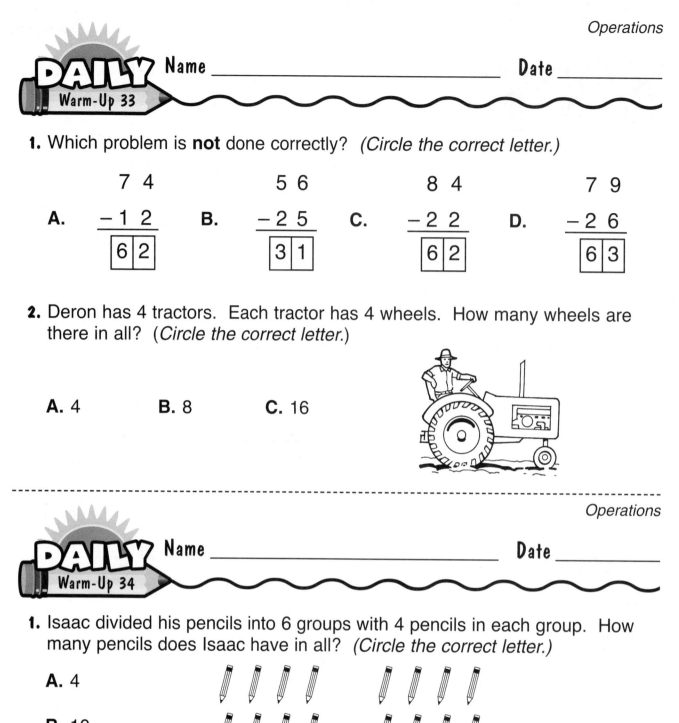

DAILY
Warm-Up 34

Name _____   **Date** _____

1. Isaac divided his pencils into 6 groups with 4 pencils in each group. How many pencils does Isaac have in all? *(Circle the correct letter.)*

A. 4

B. 10

C. 24

2. Teresa received 24 birthday gifts. She opened 19 birthday gifts. How many birthday gifts does Teresa have left to open? *(Write your answer on the line.)*

_____ birthday gifts

DAILY Warm-Up 35

Name _____ Date _____

1. Sylvester had 18 blocks. Carlos gave him some more blocks. He now has 29 blocks. How many blocks did Carlos give Sylvester? *(Write your answer on the line.)*

_____ blocks

2. Sandra grilled 24 hamburgers for her family. There were 8 hamburgers left. How many hamburgers did Sandra's family eat? *(Circle the correct letter.)*

A. 24 hamburgers

B. 32 hamburgers

C. 16 hamburgers

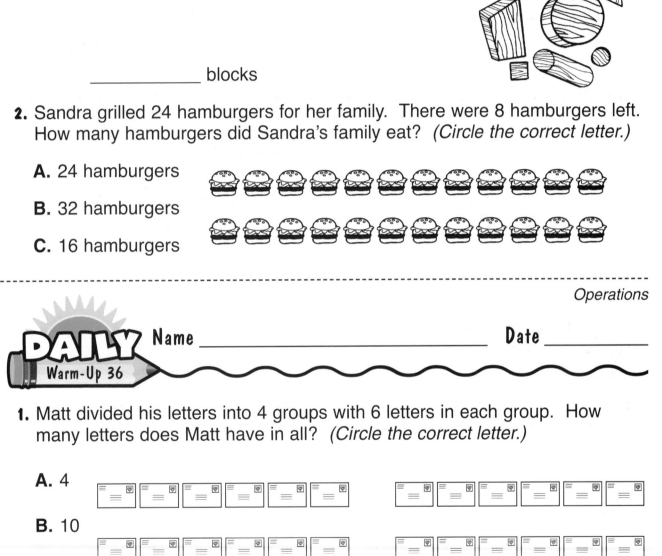

DAILY Warm-Up 36

Name _____ Date _____

1. Matt divided his letters into 4 groups with 6 letters in each group. How many letters does Matt have in all? *(Circle the correct letter.)*

A. 4

B. 10

C. 24

2. Mary has 28 dolls. She gave her friend 14 dolls. How many dolls does Mary now have? *(Write your answer on the line.)*

_____ dolls

DAILY Warm-Up 37

Name _____ Date _____

1. Kurt played soccer 43 minutes before school and 28 minutes after school. How many total minutes did Kurt play soccer? *(Write your answer on the line.)*

_____ minutes

2. Deron raises cows. He has 53 cows in his herd. Twenty-eight of the cows are white with spots. The rest are all black. How many black cows does Deron have in his herd? *(Write your answer on the line.)*

_____ black cows

DAILY Warm-Up 38

Name _____ Date _____

1. Tracy bought a book that had 80 pages. She has already read 45 pages. How many more pages does Tracy have left to read? *(Write your answer on the line.)*

_____ more pages

2. Jennifer has 12 purple T-shirts. Liz has 8 more purple T-shirts than Jennifer. How many purple T-shirts does Liz have? *(Write your answer on the line.)*

_____ purple T-shirts

DAILY Warm-Up 39

Name _____ Date _____

1. Jake put out 38 chocolate chip cookies at his party. After the party, there were only 12 cookies left. How many cookies were eaten at the party? *(Write your answer on the line.)*

_____ cookies

2. Solve the problem below. *(Write your answer in each box.)*

$$4 \times 4 = \boxed{}$$

$$4 + 4 + 4 + 4 = \boxed{}$$

DAILY Warm-Up 40

Name _____ Date _____

1. Calley has 35 fish in her fish bowl. She gave 16 fish to her best friend. How many fish does Calley now have in her fish bowl? *(Write your answer on the line.)*

_____ fish

2. Jerry had 18 baseball cards. His friend gave him some more baseball cards. He now has 29 baseball cards. How many baseball cards did Jerry's friend give him? *(Write your answer on the line.)*

_____ baseball cards

Name _____ **Date** _____

1. Mary mailed 2 letters to her friend each day for 3 days. How many letters did she mail in all? *(Write your answer in each box.)*

$$2 \times 3 = \boxed{}$$

$$2 + 2 + 2 = \boxed{}$$

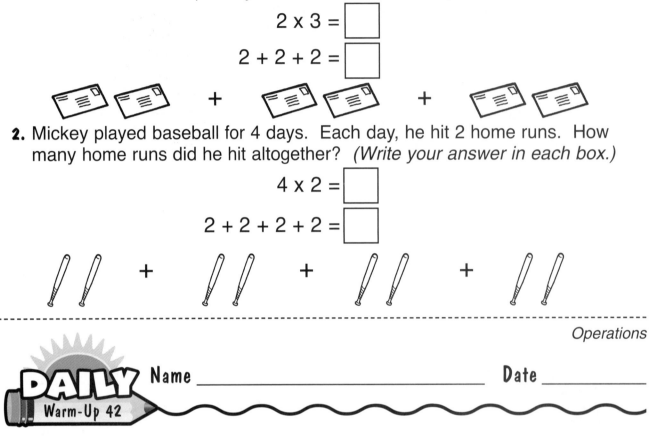

2. Mickey played baseball for 4 days. Each day, he hit 2 home runs. How many home runs did he hit altogether? *(Write your answer in each box.)*

$$4 \times 2 = \boxed{}$$

$$2 + 2 + 2 + 2 = \boxed{}$$

Name _____ **Date** _____

1. Lee saw 18 deer in a field. Six deer got scared and ran away. How many deer are still in the field? *(Write your answer on the line.)*

_____ deer

2. Shree collects bells. She has 6 bells on each of her 2 shelves. What is the total number of bells Shree has? *(Write your answer in each box.)*

$$6 \times 2 = \boxed{}$$

$$6 + 6 = \boxed{}$$

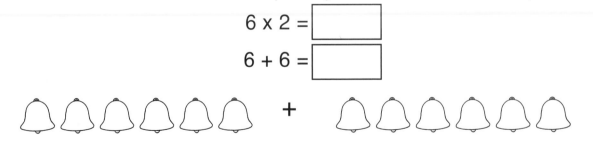

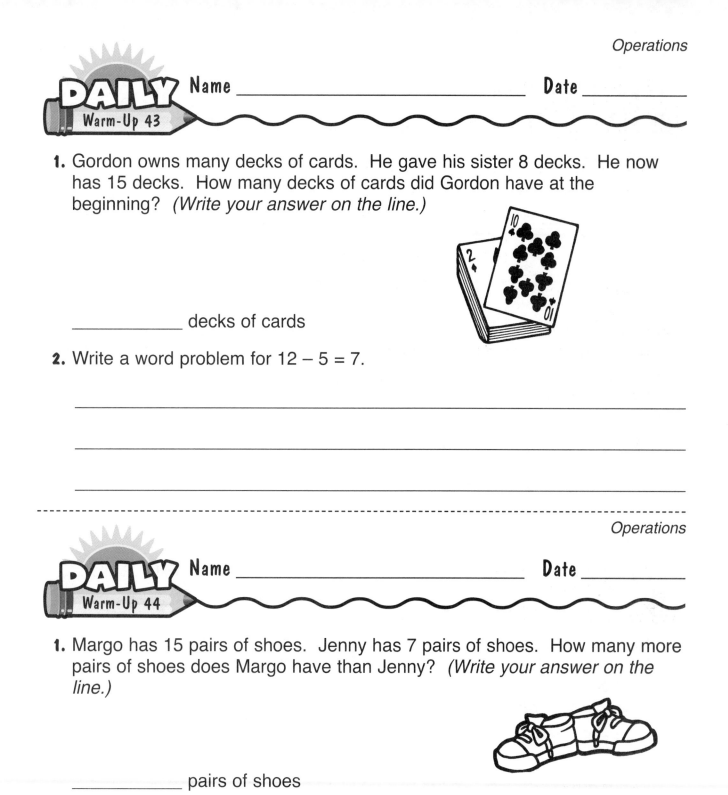

DAILY Warm-Up 43 Name _____ Date _____

1. Gordon owns many decks of cards. He gave his sister 8 decks. He now has 15 decks. How many decks of cards did Gordon have at the beginning? *(Write your answer on the line.)*

_____ decks of cards

2. Write a word problem for 12 − 5 = 7.

_____

_____

_____

- -

DAILY Warm-Up 44 Name _____ Date _____

1. Margo has 15 pairs of shoes. Jenny has 7 pairs of shoes. How many more pairs of shoes does Margo have than Jenny? *(Write your answer on the line.)*

_____ pairs of shoes

2. Solve the problems.

$$\begin{array}{cccc} 53 & 82 & 66 & 48 \\ -\,45 & +\,47 & -\,14 & +\,81 \\ \hline \end{array}$$

DAILY
Warm-Up 45

Name _____ Date _____

1. Fill in the boxes with your own numbers. Then, add or subtract.

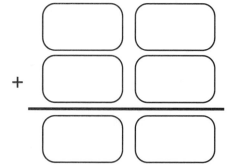

2. Mr. Hill has 16 computers that he wants to divide into 4 classrooms. How many computers will be in each classroom? (*Circle the groups of 4. Then, write your answer on the line.*)

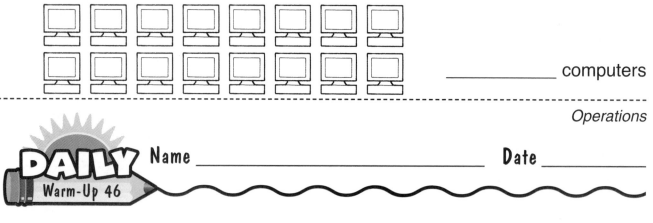

_____ computers

DAILY
Warm-Up 46

Name _____ Date _____

1. Sarah has 15 cookies she wants to share with her 3 friends. How many groups of 3 can she make so the cookies are shared equally? (*Circle the groups of 3. Then, write your answer on the line.*)

There are _____ groups of 3 in 15.

2. Mrs. Hoke has 12 flowers she wants to divide into 4 flower vases. How many flowers will be in each vase? (*Write your answer on the line.*)

_____ flowers

DAILY Warm-Up 47

Name _____ Date _____

1. Fill in the boxes with your own numbers. Then, add or subtract.

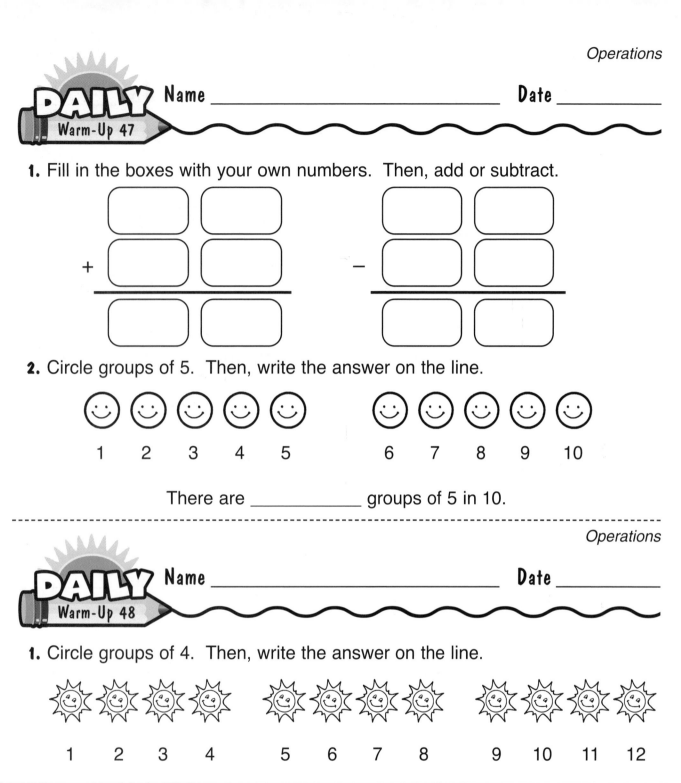

2. Circle groups of 5. Then, write the answer on the line.

1   2   3   4   5   6   7   8   9   10

There are _____ groups of 5 in 10.

DAILY Warm-Up 48

Name _____ Date _____

1. Circle groups of 4. Then, write the answer on the line.

1   2   3   4   5   6   7   8   9   10   11   12

There are _____ groups of 4 in 12.

2. Circle groups of 2. Then, write the answer on the line.

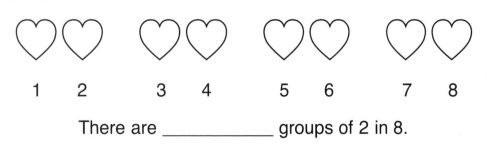

1   2   3   4   5   6   7   8

There are _____ groups of 2 in 8.

DAILY Warm-Up 49

Name _____ Date _____

1. Marcy has 3 boxes with 6 books in each box. How many total books does Marcy have? *(Write your answer on the line.)*

Marcy has _____ books.

2. Cody and Gordon each received 12 letters over the summer. How many letters did they receive together? *(Write your answer on the line.)*

_____ letters

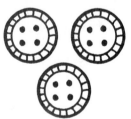

DAILY Warm-Up 50

Name _____ Date _____

1. Fanny bought 2 packages of buttons. Each package held 24 buttons. How many buttons does Fanny have in total? *(Write your answer on the line.)*

_____ buttons

2. Nancy counted 94 cows standing in a field. Thirty-eight cows got tired and laid down. How many cows are still standing? *(Write your answer on the line.)*

_____ cows are still standing.

DAILY Warm-Up 51

Name _____ Date _____

1. Kerry has 3 shelves in his bedroom. On the first shelf, he has 2 pictures. On the second shelf, he has 4 pictures, and on the third shelf he has 6 pictures. How many pictures does Kerry have in all? *(Write your answer on the line.)*

Kerry has _____ pictures.

2. The Roddy family is driving 378 miles to their home in Austin. They have already driven 143 miles. How many more miles do they have left to drive? *(Write your answer on the line.)*

_____ more miles

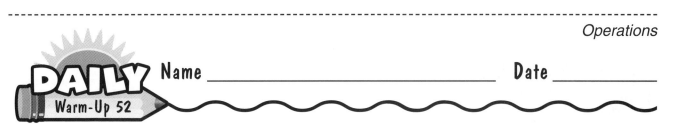

DAILY Warm-Up 52

Name _____ Date _____

1. Mary divided hair bows into 3 groups with 4 hair bows in each group. How many hair bows does Mary have in all? *(Circle the correct letter.)*

A. 1

B. 7

C. 12

2. Marco has 189 sheets of paper. This week, he used 58 sheets in school. How many sheets of paper does Marco have left? *(Write your answer on the line.)*

Marco has _____ sheets of paper left.

DAILY
Warm-Up 53

Name _____ Date _____

1. Solve the problem. *(Write your answer on the line.)*

$$4 \times 2 = \text{_____}$$

☺ ☺ ☺ ☺   +   ☺ ☺ ☺ ☺

2. Robert has 320 sports magazines. He gives 124 sports magazines to his brother. How many sports magazines does Robert now have? *(Write your answer on the line.)*

Robert has _____ sports magazines.

- -

DAILY
Warm-Up 54

Name _____ Date _____

1. Seth caught 12 worms. He wants to place an equal amount of worms in each of the 3 cans. How many worms will go in each can? *(Circle the correct letter.)*

A. 3

B. 4

C. 12

2. Sandy runs 4 miles each day. How many miles does she run in 3 days? *(Write your answer on the line.)*

Sandy runs _____ miles in 3 days.

DAILY
Warm-Up 55

Name _____   Date _____

1. Draw a line to make 2 triangles in each square.

How many triangles are there in all? There are _____ triangles.

2. There were fifteen boys and eighteen girls going on the camping trip. How many children were there in total? *(Circle the letter of the correct number sentence for this problem.)*

A. 15 − 18 =

B. 18 − 15 =

C. 15 + 18 =

DAILY
Warm-Up 56

Name _____   Date _____

1. Mike has 12 fish swimming in each of his 2 tanks. How many fish does Mike have in all? *(Circle the correct letter.)*

A. 10

B. 14

C. 24

2. Fill in the circle with the correct symbol (<, >, or =).

$$14 + 5 \bigcirc 12 + 9$$

DAILY Warm-Up 57   Name _____   Date _____

1. Carl picked eighteen carrots from his garden on Monday. On Tuesday, he picked twelve more. How many carrots did Carl pick in all? *(Circle the correct letter.)*

   A. 6

   B. 20

   C. 30

2. Jennifer had 58 papers to grade over the weekend. She has graded 23 papers. How many more papers must Jennifer grade? *(Circle the correct letter.)*

   A. 81

   B. 25

   C. 35

DAILY Warm-Up 58   Name _____   Date _____

1. Solve the problem.

   ☺ ☺ ☺ ☺

   ☺ ☺ ☺ ☺   4 x 3 = _____

   ☺ ☺ ☺ ☺

2. Elizabeth had 24 books. Her friend gave her some more. She now has 32 books. How many books did her friend give her? *(Write the answer in the box.)*

   24 + ☐ = 32

DAILY Warm-Up 59 Name _____ Date _____

1. Solve the problems.

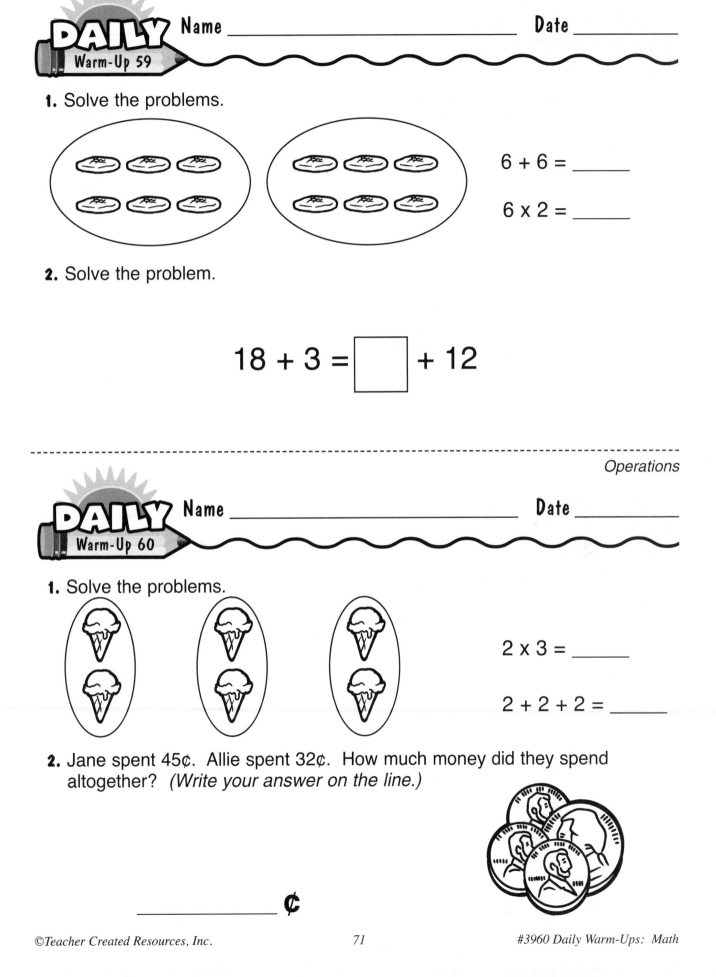

6 + 6 = _____

6 x 2 = _____

2. Solve the problem.

$$18 + 3 = \boxed{} + 12$$

DAILY Warm-Up 60 Name _____ Date _____

1. Solve the problems.

2 x 3 = _____

2 + 2 + 2 = _____

2. Jane spent 45¢. Allie spent 32¢. How much money did they spend altogether? *(Write your answer on the line.)*

_____ ¢

DAILY Warm-Up 61

Name _____ Date _____

1. Circle the pairs of numbers that add up to 15. The numbers can be adjacent to each other, vertical, horizontal, or diagonal.

7	6	9	13	12	1
10	4	2	3	14	3
5	7	1	12	11	13
9	8	6	7	13	8
10	1	7	9	2	5
11	5	6	12	3	14

2. There are 85 passengers on a plane. Five passengers can sit in each row. How many rows of seats are needed on the plane? *(Write the math problem on the line. Then solve.)*

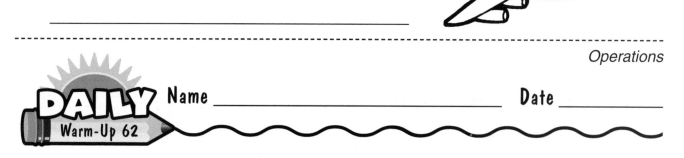

_____

DAILY Warm-Up 62

Name _____ Date _____

1. Mike drove 198 miles. The next day, he drove 89 miles. How many miles did he drive in all? *(Circle the correct letter.)*

   A. 109

   B. 207

   C. 287

2. Write a number problem about numbers on the dominoes. Then solve.

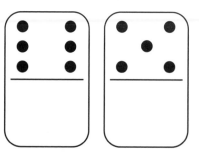

_____

Answer Key

Warm-Up 1
1. 38
2. 9

Warm-Up 2
1. C
2. 57

Warm-Up 3
1. 11, 11, 4, 7
2. 11

Warm-Up 4
1. 24
2. 24

Warm-Up 5
1. A
2. <

Warm-Up 6
1. 12
2. 24

Warm-Up 7
1. 17
2. 52

Warm-Up 8
1. 18
2. 8

Warm-Up 9
1. Sample Answer:
   $23 - 16 = 7$
2. B

Warm-Up 10
1. Numbers will vary.
2. 30

Warm-Up 11
1. 18, 18
2. 3

Warm-Up 12
1A. 6, 6
1B. 8, 8
2. 6

Warm-Up 13
1. 27
2. Answers will vary.

Warm-Up 14
1. 6
2. $\begin{array}{r} 1\ 7\ 3 \\ -\ 9\ 3 \\ \hline 8\ 0 \end{array}$

Warm-Up 15
1. 6
2. 6

Warm-Up 16
1. B
2. B

Warm-Up 17
1. $46 - 34 = 12$
2. 15

Warm-Up 18
1. 258
2. B

Warm-Up 19
1. C
2. 40

Warm-Up 20
1. 10
2. You take 34 football cards and add 9 more. The total is 43 cards.

Warm-Up 21
1. >
2. 64

Warm-Up 22
1. 18
2. 576

Warm-Up 23
1. 18
2. 88

Warm-Up 24
1. 10
2. 16

Warm-Up 25
1. 23
2. 81, 13, 127, 25

Warm-Up 26
1. A
2. 15

Warm-Up 27
1. B
2. 150, 46, 141, 56

Warm-Up 28
1. B
2. 6

Warm-Up 29
1. 14
2. <

Warm-Up 30
1. 5
2. 9

Warm-Up 31
1. C
2. 4

Warm-Up 32
1. 5
2. 103

Warm-Up 33
1. D
2. C

Warm-Up 34
1. C
2. 5

Warm-Up 35
1. 11
2. C

Warm-Up 36
1. C
2. 14

Warm-Up 37
1. 71
2. 25

Warm-Up 38
1. 35
2. 20

Warm-Up 39
1. 26
2. 16, 16

Answer Key

Warm-Up 40
1. 19
2. 11

Warm-Up 41
1. 6, 6
2. 8, 8

Warm-Up 42
1. 12
2. 12, 12

Warm-Up 43
1. 23
2. Answers will vary.

Warm-Up 44
1. 8
2. 8, 129, 52, 129

Warm-Up 45
1. Answers will vary.
2. 4

Warm-Up 46
1. 5
2. 3

Warm-Up 47
1. Answers will vary.
2. 2

Warm-Up 48
1. 3
2. 4

Warm-Up 49
1. 18
2. 24

Warm-Up 50
1. 48
2. 56

Warm-Up 51
1. 12
2. 235

Warm-Up 52
1. C
2. 131

Warm-Up 53
1. 8
2. 196

Warm-Up 54
1. B
2. 12

Warm-Up 55
1. 6
2. C

Warm-Up 56
1. C
2. <

Warm-Up 57
1. C
2. C

Warm-Up 58
1. 12
2. 8

Warm-Up 59
1. 12, 12
2. 9

Warm-Up 60
1. 6, 6
2. 77¢

Warm-Up 61
1.

2. 17 rows—$85 \div 5 = 17$

Warm-Up 62
1. C
2. Sample Answer:
   $6 + 5 = 11$

MEASUREMENT AND GEOMETRY

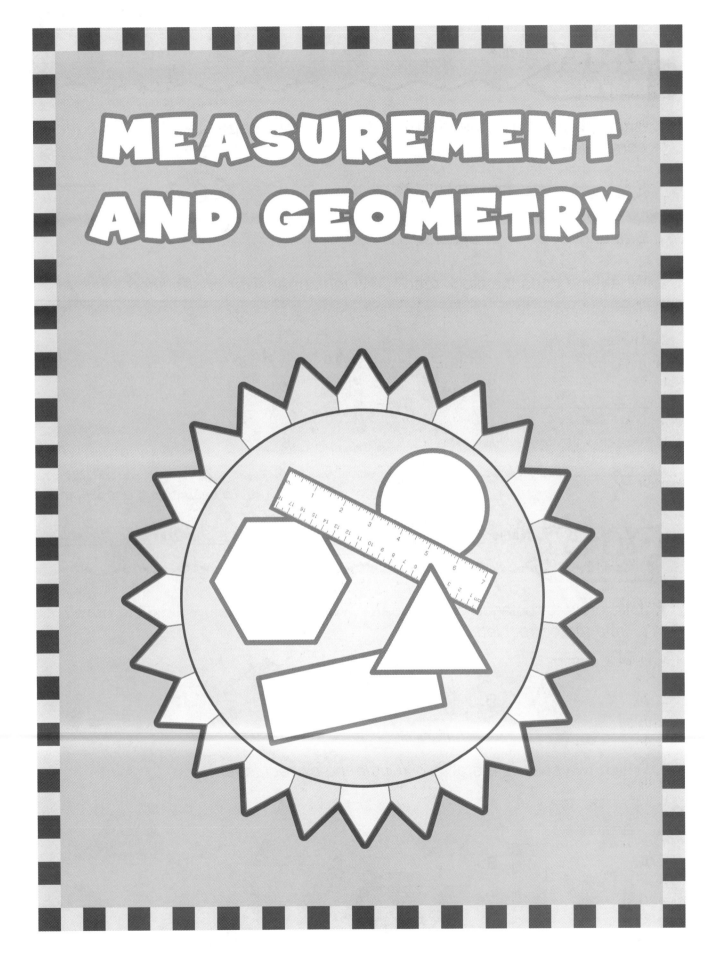

DAILY
Warm-Up 1

Name _____ Date _____

1. Jim is playing basketball. A basketball has the shape of a . . . *(Circle the correct letter.)*

   A. cube   **C.** circle

   B. triangle   **D.** sphere

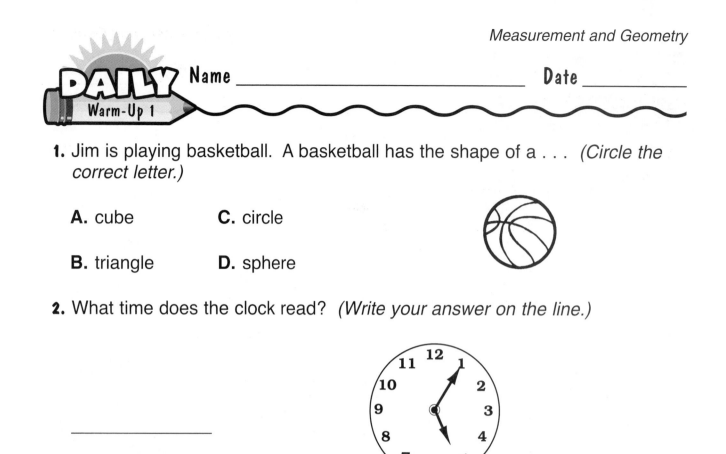

2. What time does the clock read? *(Write your answer on the line.)*

   _____

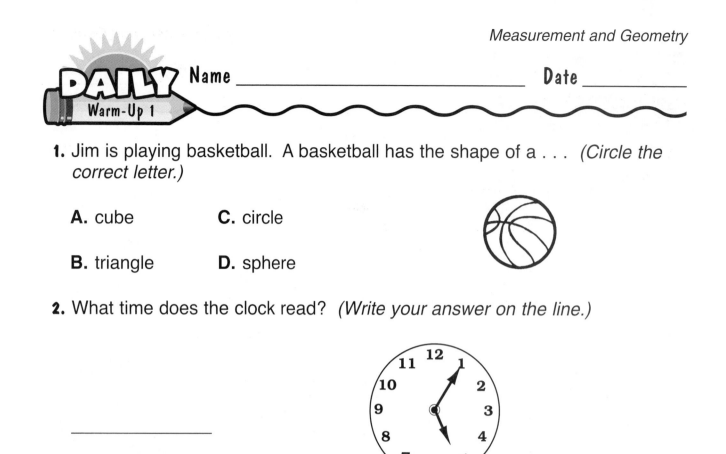

DAILY
Warm-Up 2

Name _____ Date _____

1. Jake drew an octagon on the board. Which shape below did Jake draw? *(Circle the correct letter.)*

   A.   **B.**   **C.**   **D.**

2. Which two shapes are alike? *(Circle the correct letter.)*

   A.   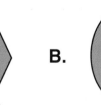   **B.**   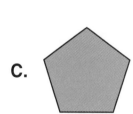   **C.**   **D.**

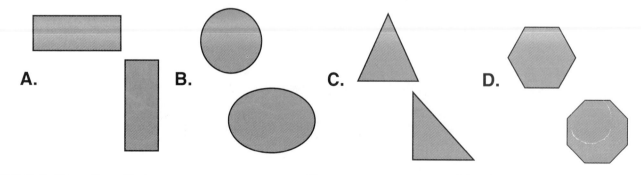

Name _____   **Date** _____

1. About how many centimeters long is the pencil? *(Write your answer on the line.)*

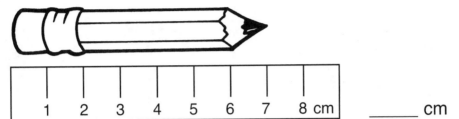

_____ cm

2. Which clock below reads 10:45? *(Circle the correct letter.)*

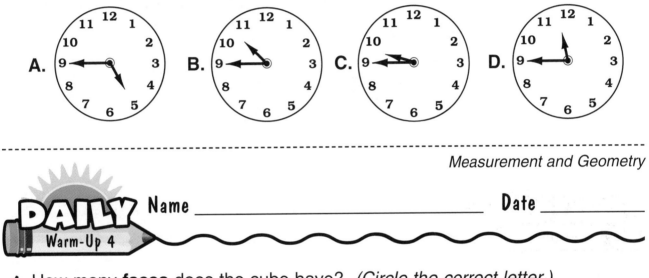

A.   B.   C.   D.

Name _____   **Date** _____

1. How many **faces** does the cube have? *(Circle the correct letter.)*

A. 2   **C.** 6

B. 4   **D.** 8

2. Are the letters alike or different? *(Circle the correct answer.)*

Alike   **Different**

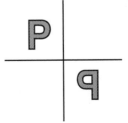

DAILY Warm-Up 5   Name _____   Date _____

1. Which shape does **not** show a line of symmetry drawn correctly? *(Circle the correct letter.)*

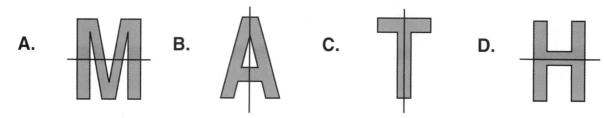

A. M   **B.** A   **C.** T   **D.** H

2. Look at the two clocks. Show 10 minutes later on the second clock.

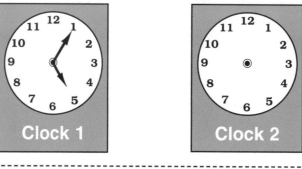

Clock 1   Clock 2

DAILY Warm-Up 6   Name _____   Date _____

1. Which geometric figure is the can of soda? *(Circle the correct letter.)*

A. cube   **C.** cylinder

B. cone   **D.** circle

2. Read the time on the clocks. Show 15 minutes later on all four clocks.

4:10	1:15	2:30	5:20
A.	**B.**	**C.**	**D.**

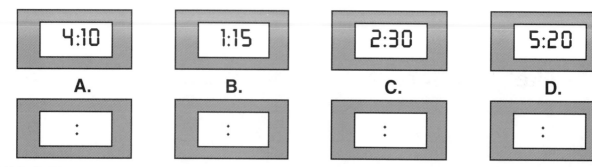

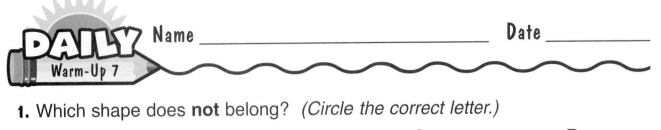

DAILY Warm-Up 7   Name _____   Date _____

1. Which shape does **not** belong? *(Circle the correct letter.)*

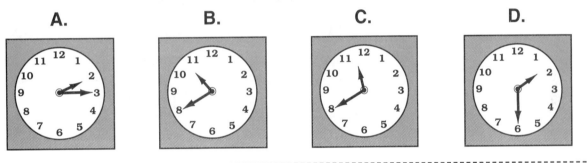

| A. | B. | C. | D. |

2. What time shows 10:40? *(Circle the correct letter.)*

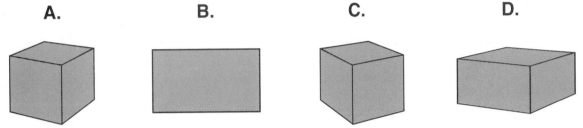

| A. | B. | C. | D. |

DAILY Warm-Up 8   Name _____   Date _____

1. Which object is a cone? *(Circle the correct letter.)*

A.   B.   C.

2. Which object is a square? *(Circle the correct letter.)*

A.   B.

DAILY Warm-Up 9

Name _____ Date _____

1. How many more grams does it take to balance the scale? *(Write your answer on the line.)*

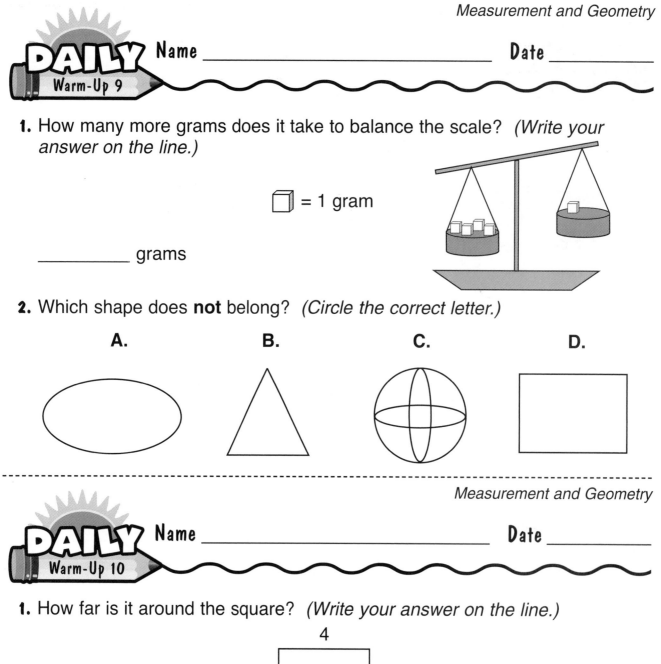

□ = 1 gram

_____ grams

2. Which shape does **not** belong? *(Circle the correct letter.)*

A.   B.   C.   D.

DAILY Warm-Up 10

Name _____ Date _____

1. How far is it around the square? *(Write your answer on the line.)*

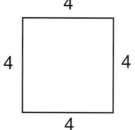

4
4   4
4

_____

2. Peggy used three types of ribbon for a project. How much ribbon of each kind did she use? *(Write your answers on the lines.)*

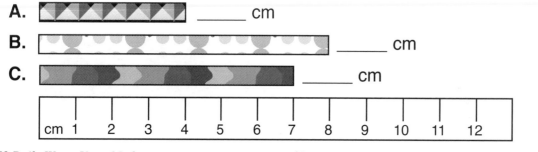

A. _____ cm

B. _____ cm

C. _____ cm

cm 1 2 3 4 5 6 7 8 9 10 11 12

Measurement and Geometry

DAILY Warm-Up 11 Name ______________________ Date __________

1. Which shape below could be made by putting together the two triangles below? *(Circle the correct letter.)*

A. rectangle

B. cube

C. square

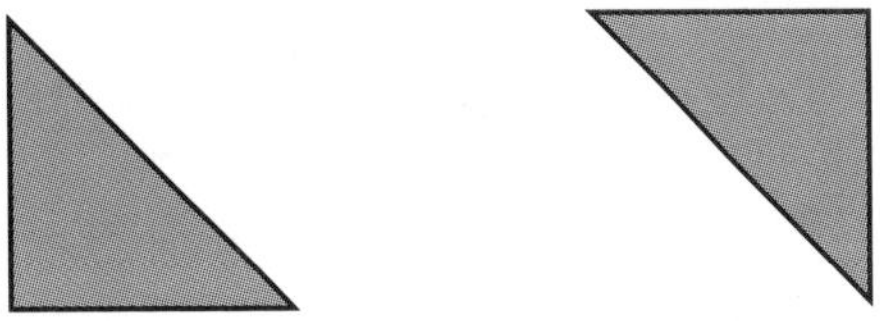

2. Write the answers on the lines.

There are _________ days in a week.

There are _________ minutes in an hour.

Measurement and Geometry

DAILY Warm-Up 12 Name ______________________ Date __________

1. Look at both clocks. How many minutes have passed? *(Circle the correct letter.)*

A. 25 minutes

B. 30 minutes

C. 35 minutes

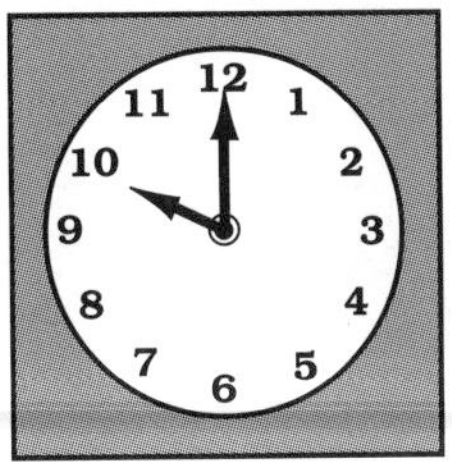

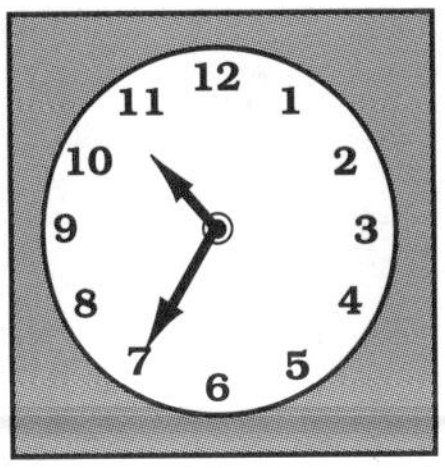

2. Circle the letter of the container that holds 4 quarts of liquid.

A.

B.

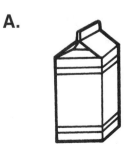

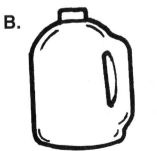

C.

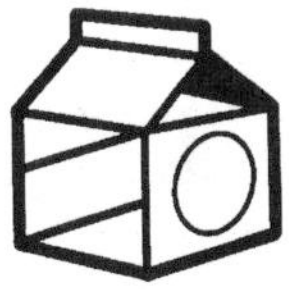

DAILY Warm-Up 13

Name _____ Date _____

1. Are both sides the same? *(Circle the correct answers.)*

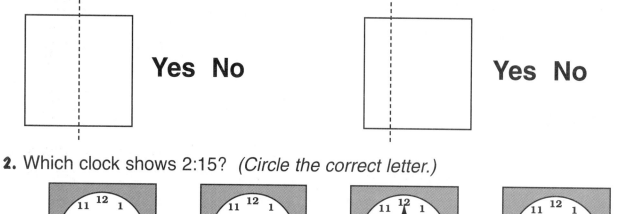

Yes No   Yes No

2. Which clock shows 2:15? *(Circle the correct letter.)*

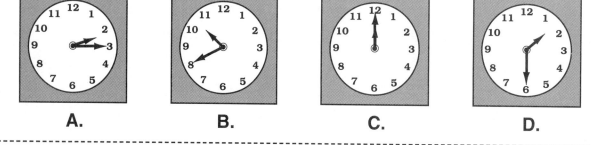

A.   B.   C.   D.

DAILY Warm-Up 14

Name _____ Date _____

1. Describe how the two shapes are different.

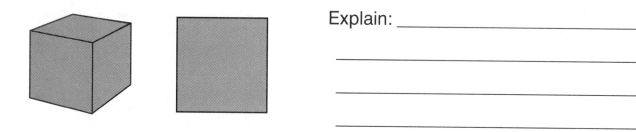

Explain: _____

_____

_____

_____

2. Which shape is a sphere? *(Circle the correct letter.)*

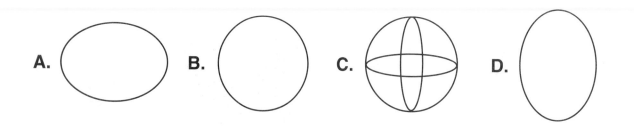

A.   B.   C.   D.

DAILY Warm-Up 15

Name _____   **Date** _____

1. Last year, Ty was 56 inches tall. This year Ty is 6 inches taller. How many inches tall is Ty this year? *(Write your answer on the line.)*

_____ inches

2. Deron mowed his yard. The clocks show the time he started and finished. How long did it take Deron to mow his yard? *(Write your answer on the line.)*

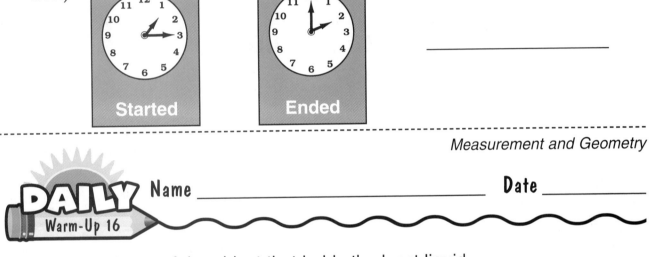

Started   Ended

_____

DAILY Warm-Up 16

Name _____   **Date** _____

1. Circle the letter of the object that holds the least liquid.

A.   **B.**   **C.**

2. Monica needs to put water in the vase. Should she use pints or liters to measure the amount of water the vase holds? *(Circle the correct answer.)*

pints   liters

DAILY Name _____ Date _____
Warm-Up 17

1. Mrs. Watkins drew the figure below on the board. She asked a student if the figure had at least one line of symmetry. If the student answered correctly, what answer did the student give? *(Circle the correct answer.)*

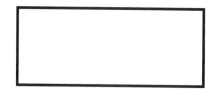

Yes   No

2. A square has four corners and four sides. *(Circle the correct answer.)*

True   False

DAILY Name _____ Date _____
Warm-Up 18

1. Linda drew two shapes on the chalkboard. What two shapes did she draw? *(Circle the correct letter.)*

A. octagon and pentagon

B. pentagon and cube

C. circle and hexagon

D. pentagon and hexagon

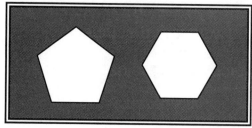

2. Estimate how many faces long the paintbrush is. *(Write your estimate on the line.)*

_____ smiley faces long

DAILY
Warm-Up 19

Name _____ Date _____

1. Which can be used to measure length? *(Circle the correct letter.)*

A. [ruler cm 1 2 3 4 5 6 7 8 9 10 11 12]

B. [clock]

C. [thermometer]

2. Look at the balance scale. How much do the scissors weigh? *(Circle the correct letter.)*

A. 20 grams

B. 10 grams

C. 30 grams

Weighs 20 grams

Weighs 10 grams

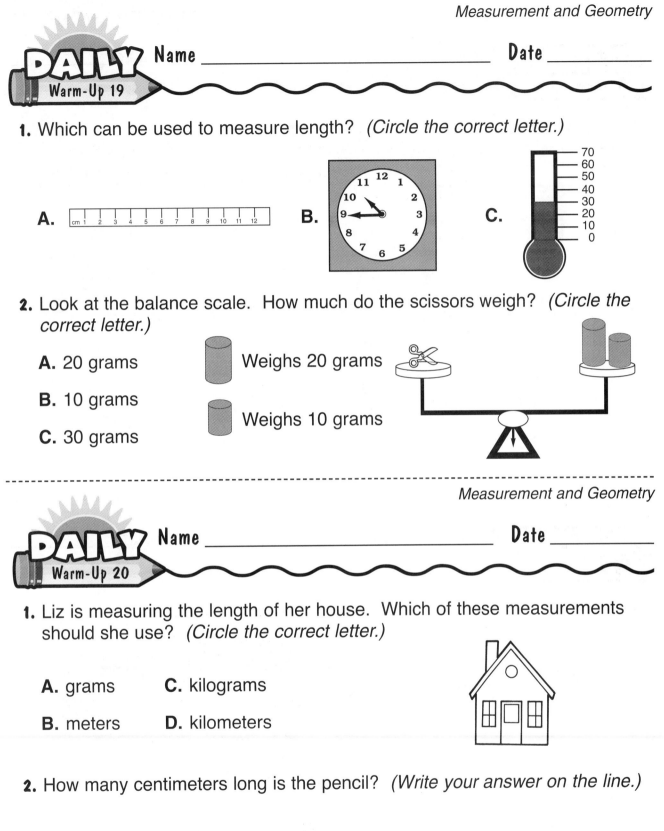

DAILY
Warm-Up 20

Name _____ Date _____

1. Liz is measuring the length of her house. Which of these measurements should she use? *(Circle the correct letter.)*

A. grams   **C.** kilograms

B. meters   **D.** kilometers

2. How many centimeters long is the pencil? *(Write your answer on the line.)*

_____ cm

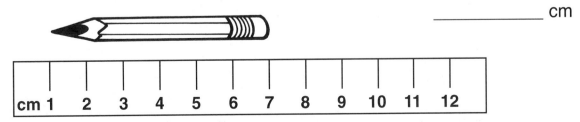

cm 1 2 3 4 5 6 7 8 9 10 11 12

DAILY Warm-Up 21

Name _____   Date _____

1. Which can be used to measure temperature? *(Circle the correct letter.)*

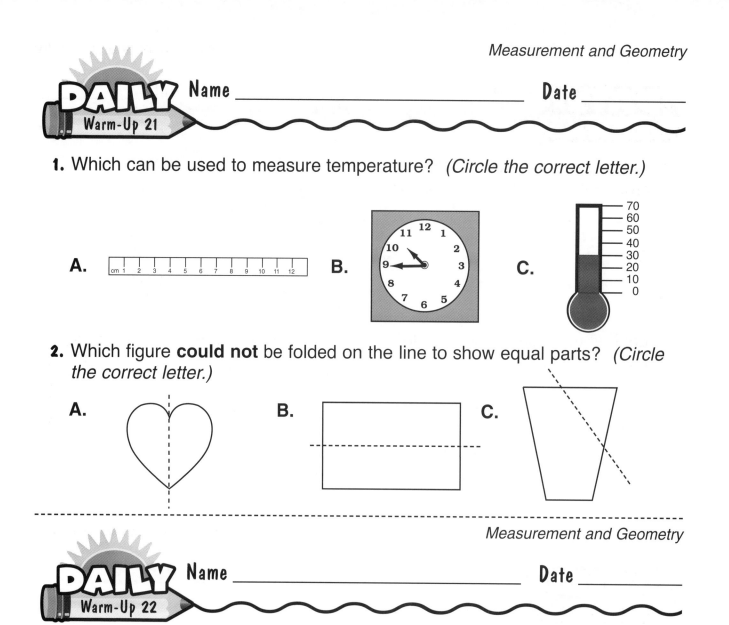

A.   **B.**   **C.**

2. Which figure **could not** be folded on the line to show equal parts? *(Circle the correct letter.)*

A.   **B.**   **C.**

- -

DAILY Warm-Up 22

Name _____   Date _____

1. Which object holds the most liquid? *(Circle the correct letter.)*

A.   **B.**   **C.**

2. How many centimeters long is the tool? *(Write your answer on the line.)*

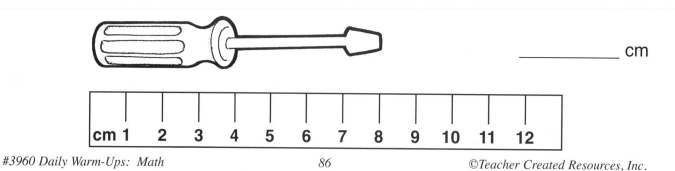

_____ cm

DAILY Warm-Up 23

Name _____ Date _____

1. Reba is having a pool put in her back yard. How many feet are there around the pool? *(Write your answer on the line.)*

9 ft.

5 ft.   5 ft.   _____ feet

9 ft.

2. Use the calendar to answer the question.

Today is May 3rd. Jake's birthday is on May 19th. How many more days until Jake's birthday?

_____ days

May 2004						
SUNDAY	MONDAY	TUESDAY	WEDNESDAY	THURSDAY	FRIDAY	SATURDAY
1	2	3	4	5	6	7
8	9	10	11	12	13	14
15	16	17	18	19	20	21
22	23	24	25	26	27	28
29	30	31				

DAILY Warm-Up 24

Name _____ Date _____

1. How many grams does the bottle of glue weigh? *(Circle the correct letter.)*

A. 12 grams

B. 8 grams   ▢ = 2 grams

C. 6 grams

2. How many cubes long is the tool below? *(Write your answer on the line.)*

_____ cubes

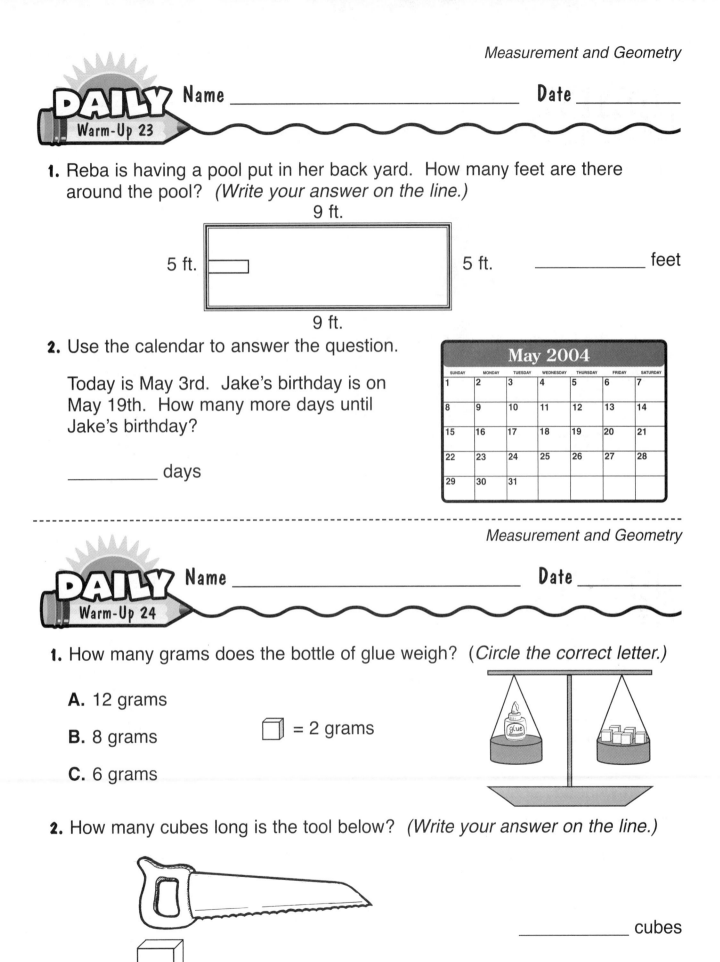

Name _____ **Date** _____

1. How many sides does this shape have? *(Write your answer on the line.)*

_____ sides

2. Use the letters in the key to name the shapes below.

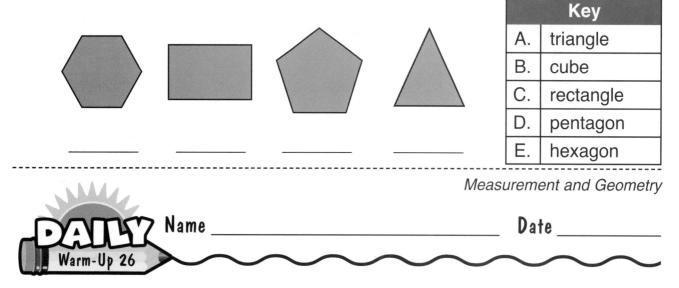

Key	
A.	triangle
B.	cube
C.	rectangle
D.	pentagon
E.	hexagon

_____   _____   _____

- -

Name _____ **Date** _____

1. Answer the questions below using the calendar.

What is the name of the month?

_____

How many days are in this month?

_____

On what day of the week is the 26th?

_____

May 2004

SUNDAY	MONDAY	TUESDAY	WEDNESDAY	THURSDAY	FRIDAY	SATURDAY
1	2	3	4	5	6	7
8	9	10	11	12	13	14
15	16	17	18	19	20	21
22	23	24	25	26	27	28
29	30	31				

2. How many centimeters long is the pencil? *(Write your answer on the line.)*

_____ cm

cm 1   2   3   4   5   6   7   8   9   10   11   12

DAILY
Warm-Up 27

Name _____ Date _____

1. Is this a line of symmetry? *(Circle the correct answer.)*

Yes   No

2. Which shape is a solid? *(Circle the correct letter.)*

A.   B.   C.   D.

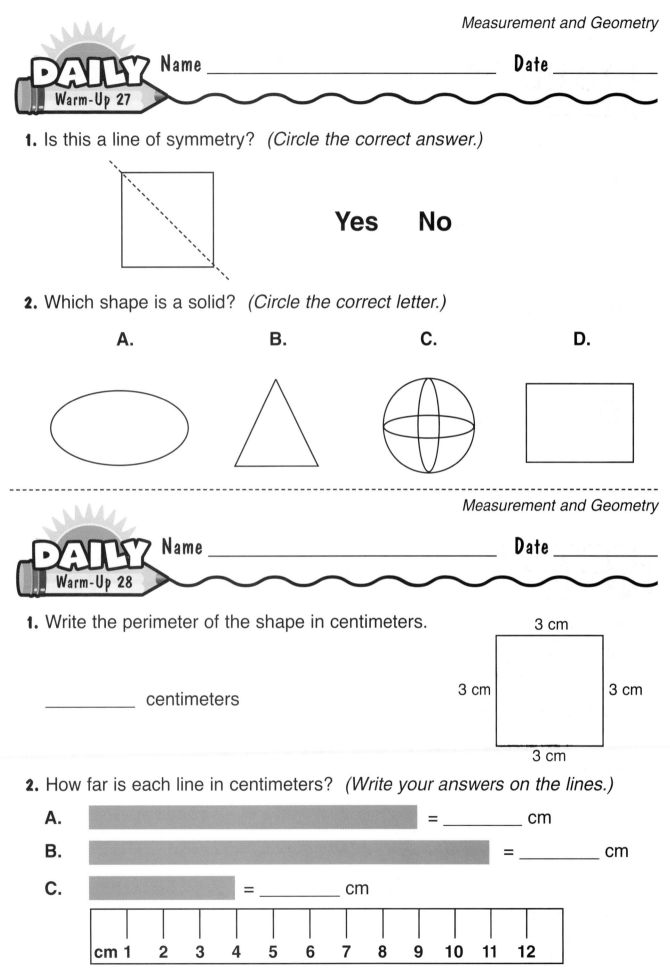

DAILY
Warm-Up 28

Name _____ Date _____

1. Write the perimeter of the shape in centimeters.

3 cm

3 cm   3 cm

_____ centimeters

3 cm

2. How far is each line in centimeters? *(Write your answers on the lines.)*

A.   = _____ cm

B.   = _____ cm

C.   = _____ cm

cm 1   2   3   4   5   6   7   8   9   10   11   12

DAILY Name _____   Date _____
Warm-Up 29

1. Are both sides the same? *(Circle the correct answer.)*

Yes   No

2. Which clock shows 1:30? *(Circle the correct letter.)*

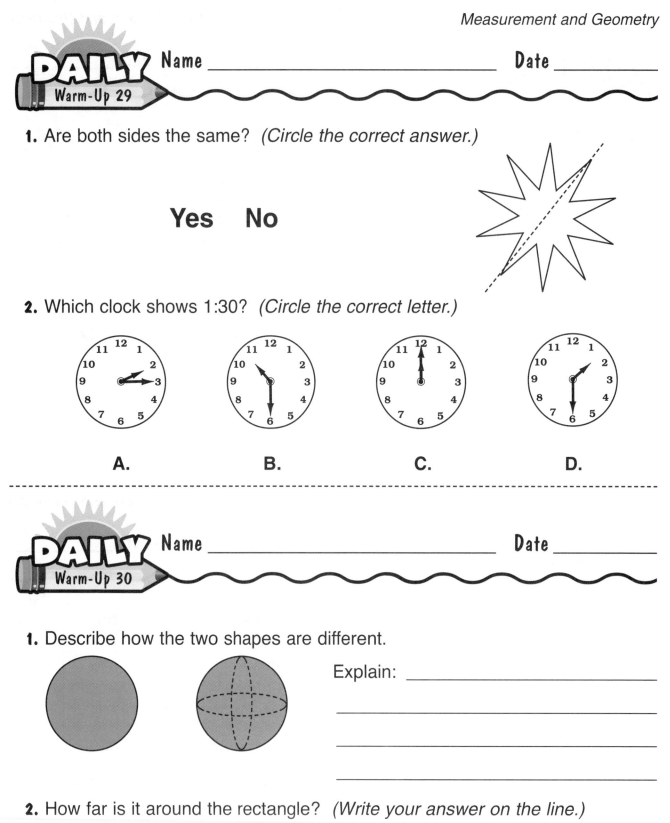

A.   **B.**   **C.**   **D.**

- -

DAILY Name _____   Date _____
Warm-Up 30

1. Describe how the two shapes are different.

Explain: _____

_____

_____

_____

2. How far is it around the rectangle? *(Write your answer on the line.)*

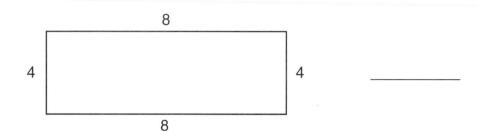

8

4   4   _____

8

DAILY
Warm-Up 31

Name _____ Date _____

1. Which shape has a line of symmetry drawn correctly? *(Circle the correct letter.)*

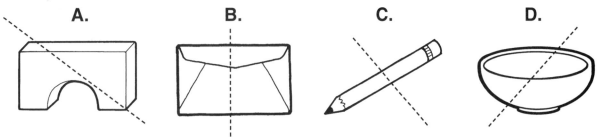

A.   B.   C.   D.

2. Draw the clock hands to show 10:15.

- -

DAILY
Warm-Up 32

Name _____ Date _____

1. This shape is a cylinder. *(Circle the correct answer.)*

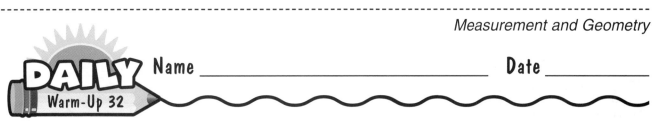

True   **False**

2. Look at each clock. Draw clock hands showing the correct time under each clock.

 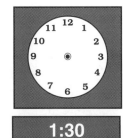  

| 3:40 | 1:30 | 12:00 | 3:15 |

DAILY Name _____ **Date** _____
Warm-Up 33

1. A square is a plane figure with four equal sides. *(Circle the correct answer.)*

Yes   No

2. Draw the clocks' hands to show the time under each clock.

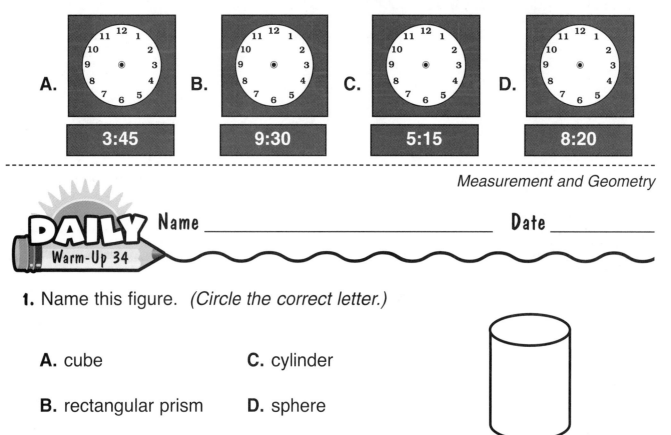

A. 3:45   **B.** 9:30   **C.** 5:15   **D.** 8:20

DAILY Name _____ **Date** _____
Warm-Up 34

1. Name this figure. *(Circle the correct letter.)*

A. cube   **C.** cylinder

B. rectangular prism   **D.** sphere

2. Which is **not** an example of a slide? *(Circle the correct letter.)*

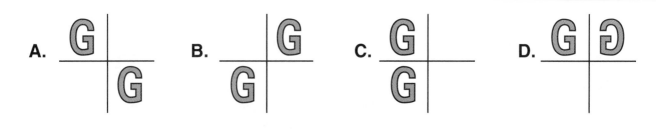

A.   **B.**   **C.**   **D.**

DAILY
Warm-Up 35

Name _____   Date _____

1. Answer **true** or **false** to the problems below.

A full bathtub holds less than 1 gallon.   **True   False**

A glass of water is less than 1 gallon.   **True   False**

1 gallon = 4 quarts

2. How heavy is the watermelon? *(Circle the correct letter.)*

A. 6 feet   **B.** 6 gallons   **C.** 6 pounds

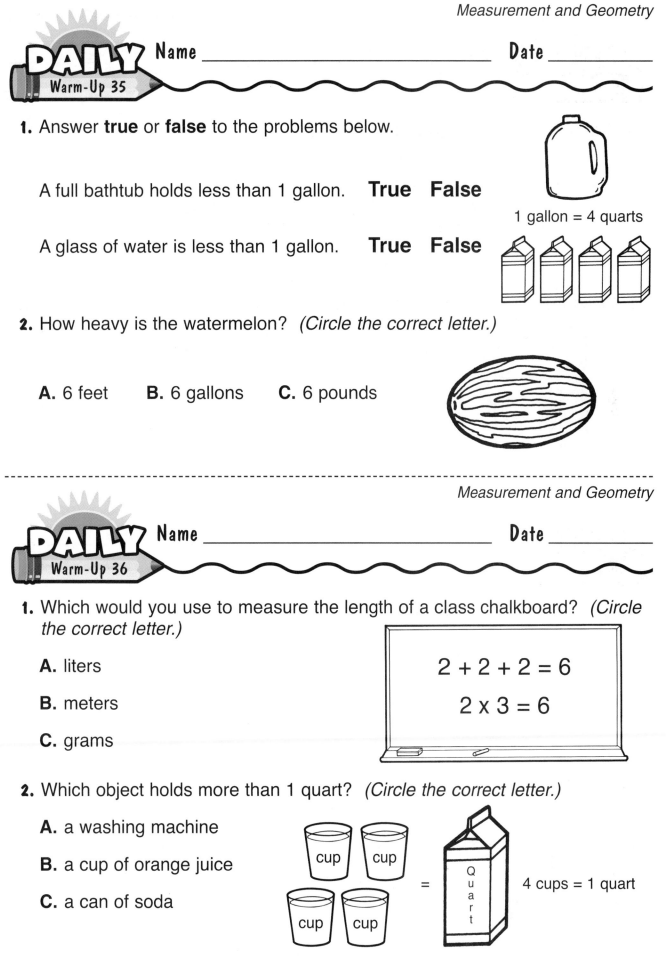

DAILY
Warm-Up 36

Name _____   Date _____

1. Which would you use to measure the length of a class chalkboard? *(Circle the correct letter.)*

A. liters

B. meters

C. grams

2 + 2 + 2 = 6

2 x 3 = 6

2. Which object holds more than 1 quart? *(Circle the correct letter.)*

A. a washing machine

B. a cup of orange juice

C. a can of soda

cup   cup
cup   cup
= Quart

4 cups = 1 quart

Name _____ **Date** _____

1. Are the two shapes below alike or different? *(Circle the correct answer.)*

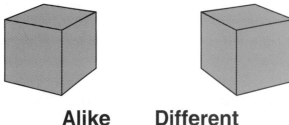

Alike   Different

2. Circle the letter of the object that would be best to measure the weight of a pair of shoes.

A.

B. | 1 | 2 | 3 | 4 | 5 | 6 | 7 | 8 cm |

Name _____ **Date** _____

1. Are the two figures congruent? *(Circle the correct answer.)*

Yes

No

2. Answer the questions below.

How many corners? _____

How many sides? _____

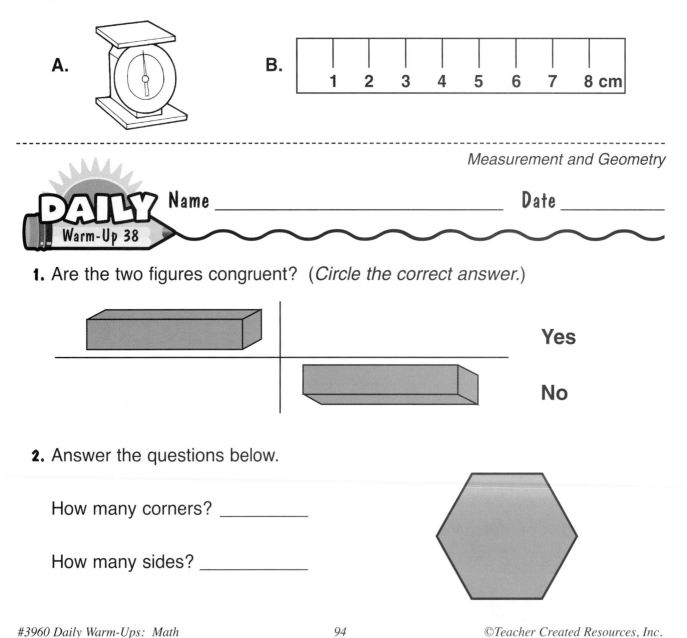

DAILY Warm-Up 39 Name _____ Date _____

1. Match the plane shapes with the correct letters. The first one is done for you.

rectangle ___**B**___

triangle _____

circle _____

square _____

A. ▪ (square)

C. ● (circle)

B. ▬ (rectangle)

D. ◣ (triangle)

2. Match the solid shapes with the correct letters.

cube _____

rectangular prism _____

sphere _____

cylinder _____

A. (cube)

C. (sphere)

B. (rectangular prism)

D. (cylinder)

DAILY Warm-Up 40 Name _____ Date _____

1. Sandra, Liz, and Teresa all drew shapes on the board. Who drew a shape with the most sides? *(Circle the correct letter.)*

A. Sandra

B. Teresa

C. Liz

Liz (hexagon)   Teresa (octagon)   Sandra (pentagon)

2. A movie started at 2:15. It ended two hours later. Show what time the movie ended.

Started

Ended

Name _____   **Date** _____

Warm-Up 41

1. The larger rectangle is 20 centimeters long.   How long is the smaller rectangle?   *(Circle the correct letter.)*

A. 20 centimeters

B. 10 centimeters

C. 30 centimeters

2. Draw hands on the clock showing 3:15.

Name _____   **Date** _____

Warm-Up 42

1. The Computer Club meets every Thursday. How many times will they meet in this month of March?   *(Circle the correct letter.)*

A. 4   **B.** 5   **C.** 6

March 2004						
SUNDAY	MONDAY	TUESDAY	WEDNESDAY	THURSDAY	FRIDAY	SATURDAY
		1	2	3	4	5
6	7	8	9	10	11	12
13	14	15	16	17	18	19
20	21	22	23	24	25	26
27	28	29	30	31		

2. James put a cylinder on a sheet of paper.   He drew around the bottom of the cylinder.   Which picture shows what shape he made?   *(Circle the correct letter.)*

A.   **B.**   **C.**

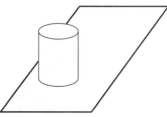

DAILY
Warm-Up 43

Name _____ Date _____

1. Which tool is the best to see how tall a door is? *(Circle the correct letter.)*

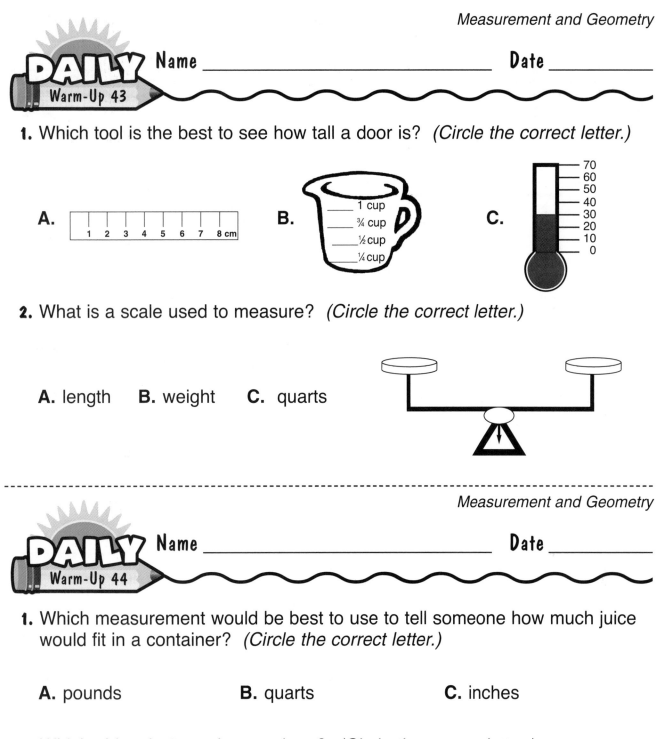

A. 1 2 3 4 5 6 7 8 cm

B. 1 cup ¾ cup ½ cup ¼ cup

C. 70 60 50 40 30 20 10 0

2. What is a scale used to measure? *(Circle the correct letter.)*

A. length   **B.** weight   **C.** quarts

DAILY
Warm-Up 44

Name _____ Date _____

1. Which measurement would be best to use to tell someone how much juice would fit in a container? *(Circle the correct letter.)*

A. pounds   **B.** quarts   **C.** inches

2. Which object is 3 centimeters long? *(Circle the correct letter.)*

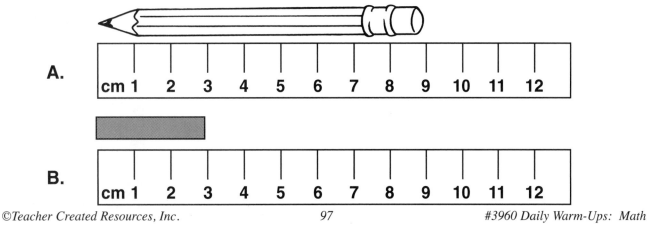

A. cm 1 2 3 4 5 6 7 8 9 10 11 12

B. cm 1 2 3 4 5 6 7 8 9 10 11 12

DAILY
Warm-Up 45

Name _____ Date _____

1. Which names the object? *(Circle the correct letter.)*

A. cone   **B.** rectangular prism   **C.** sphere

2. What time does the clock read? *(Circle the correct letter.)*

A. 4:05   **B.** 5:05   **C.** 6:05

DAILY
Warm-Up 46

Name _____ Date _____

1. Is this a line of symmetry? *(Circle the correct answer.)*

Yes   **No**

2. What does the thermometer read?
(Circle the correct letter.)

A. 40° F   **B.** 60° F   **C.** 70° F

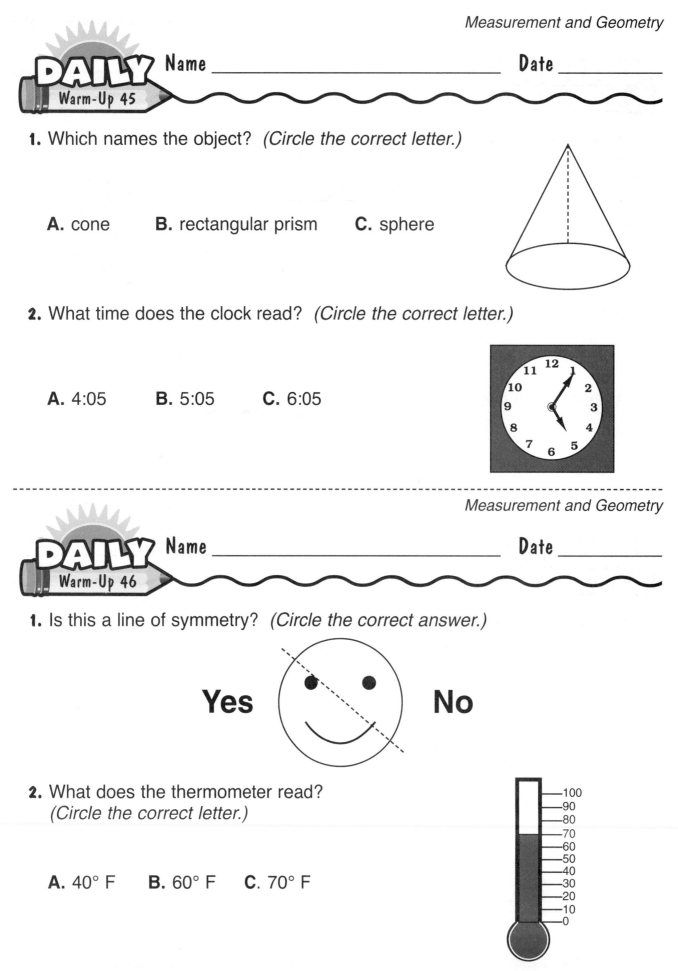

DAILY Name _____ Date _____

Warm-Up 47

1. Which shape is the same size and shape as the shaded figure? *(Circle the correct letter.)*

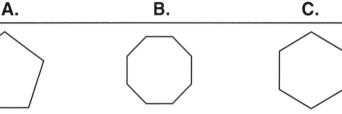

| | **A.** | **B.** | **C.** |

2. Look at the two clocks. Show 15 minutes later on the second clock.

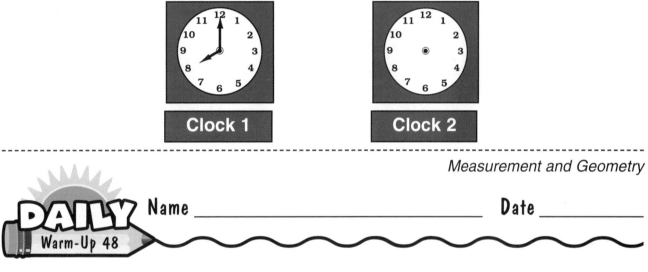

Clock 1   Clock 2

DAILY Name _____ Date _____

Warm-Up 48

1. How far is it around the square? *(Write your answer on the line.)*

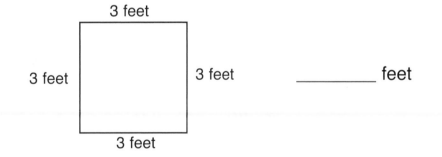

3 feet

3 feet   3 feet   _____ feet

3 feet

2. About how many centimeters long is the rectangle? *(Write your answer on the line.)*

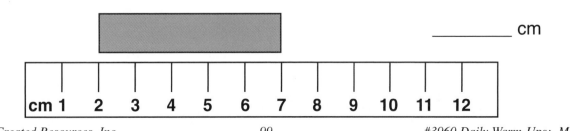

_____ cm

cm 1 2 3 4 5 6 7 8 9 10 11 12

DAILY Warm-Up 49

Name _____ Date _____

1. Is this a line of symmetry? *(Circle "Yes" or "No.")*

Yes 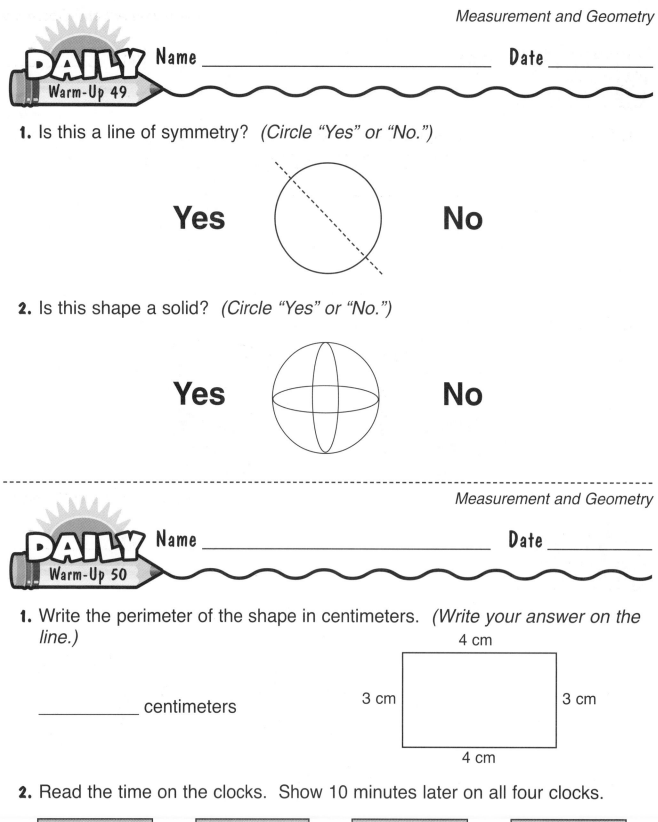 **No**

2. Is this shape a solid? *(Circle "Yes" or "No.")*

Yes **No**

DAILY Warm-Up 50

Name _____ Date _____

1. Write the perimeter of the shape in centimeters. *(Write your answer on the line.)*

4 cm

3 cm 3 cm

_____ centimeters

4 cm

2. Read the time on the clocks. Show 10 minutes later on all four clocks.

 2:10

 3:15

 4:45

 6:20

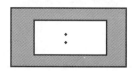

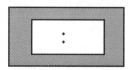

DAILY Warm-Up 51

Name _____ **Date** _____

1. Explain how these shapes are different.

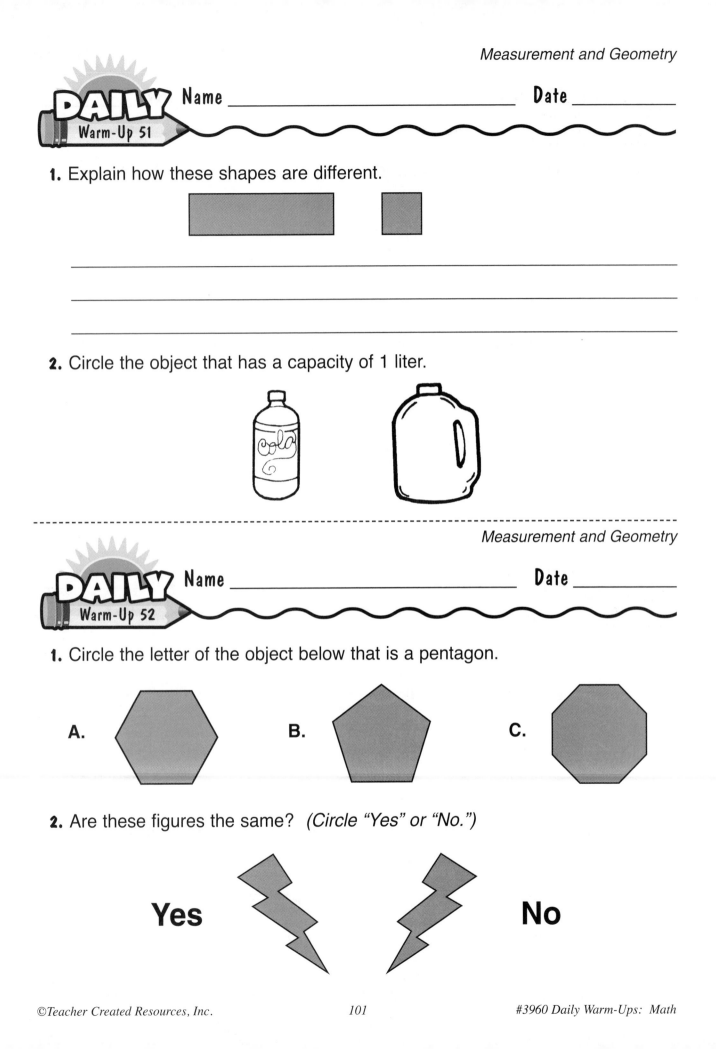

_____

_____

_____

2. Circle the object that has a capacity of 1 liter.

DAILY Warm-Up 52

Name _____ **Date** _____

1. Circle the letter of the object below that is a pentagon.

A.   **B.**   **C.**

2. Are these figures the same? *(Circle "Yes" or "No.")*

Yes   **No**

DAILY
Warm-Up 53

Name _____ Date _____

1. How long will it take to count from 1 to 20? *(Circle the correct letter.)*

    A. hours   **B.** minutes   **C.** seconds

2. About how long would it take to see a movie at a theater? *(Circle the correct letter.)*

    A. hours   **B.** minutes   **C.** seconds

DAILY
Warm-Up 54

Name _____ Date _____

1. Which shape is **not** the same on each side? *(Circle the correct letter.)*

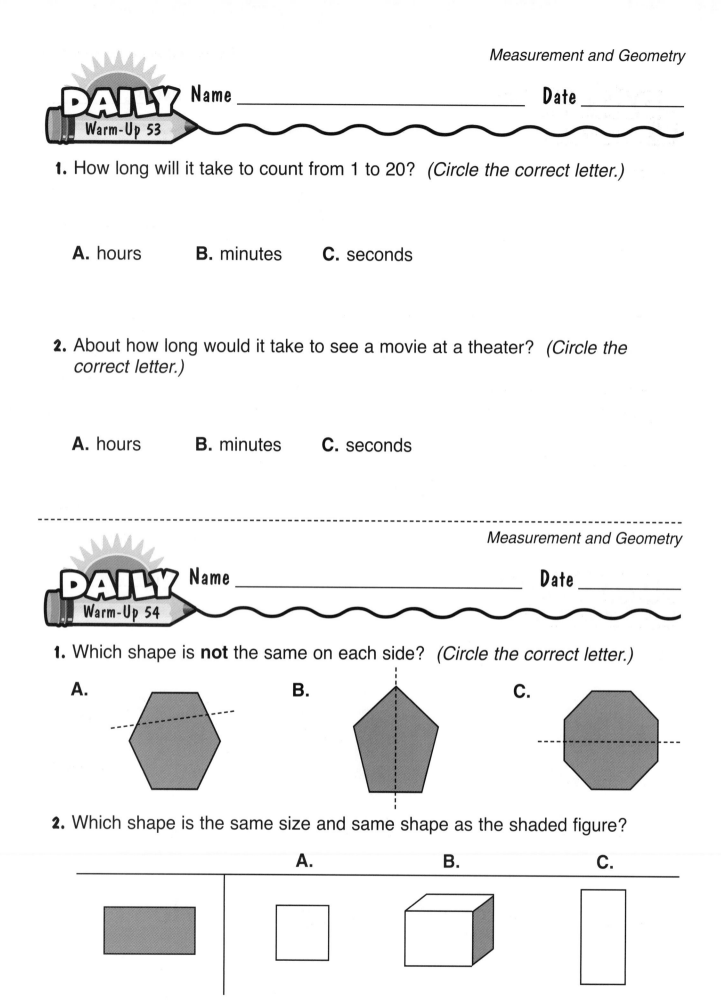

A.   **B.**   **C.**

2. Which shape is the same size and same shape as the shaded figure?

                        A.   **B.**   **C.**

DAILY
Warm-Up 55

Name _____   Date _____

1. Explain what is different about the two shapes.

_____

_____

_____

_____

2. Use this calendar to answer the question.

How many even days are in the
month of June?

_____ days

June 2004

SUNDAY	MONDAY	TUESDAY	WEDNESDAY	THURSDAY	FRIDAY	SATURDAY
1	2	3	4	5	6	7
8	9	10	11	12	13	14
15	16	17	18	19	20	21
22	23	24	25	26	27	28
29	30					

DAILY
Warm-Up 56

Name _____   Date _____

1. How many grams is the wrench? *(Circle the correct letter.)*

A. 3 grams

B. 10 grams   = 10 grams

C. 30 grams

2. How long would it take boil an egg? *(Circle the correct letter.)*

A. hours   **B.** minutes   **C.** seconds

DAILY
Warm-Up 57

Name _____   Date _____

1. About how many jellybeans will a small baby jar hold?
(Circle the correct letter.)

A. 1,000   **B.** 500   **C.** 50

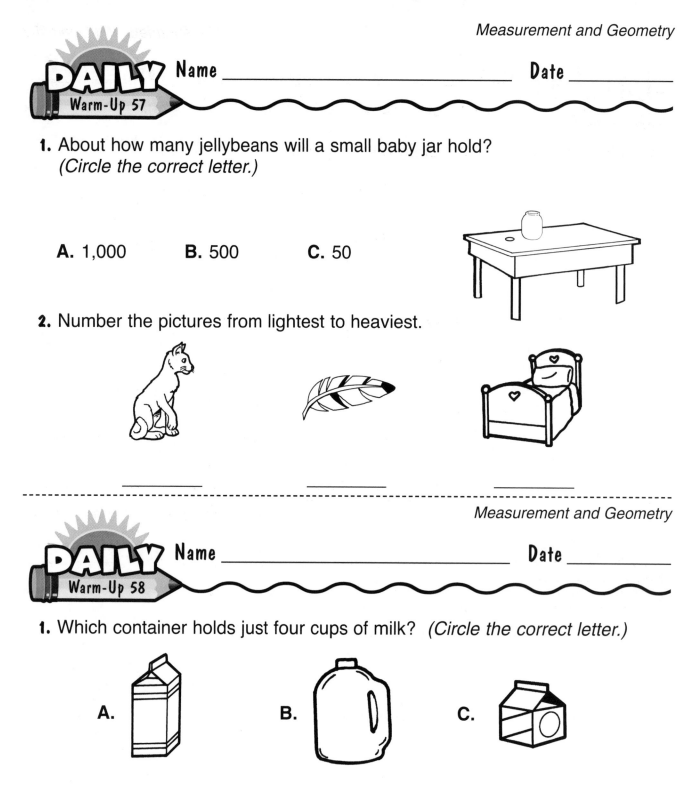

2. Number the pictures from lightest to heaviest.

_____   _____   _____

DAILY
Warm-Up 58

Name _____   Date _____

1. Which container holds just four cups of milk? *(Circle the correct letter.)*

A.   **B.**   **C.**

2. Draw a line of symmetry on the figure.

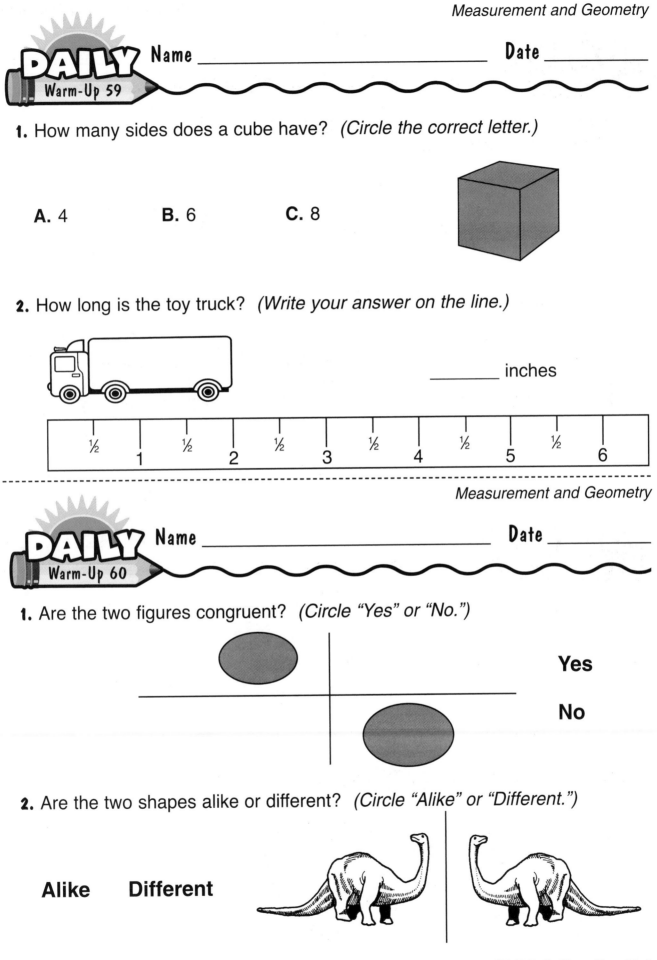

DAILY Warm-Up 59

Name _____ Date _____

1. How many sides does a cube have? *(Circle the correct letter.)*

A. 4   **B.** 6   **C.** 8

2. How long is the toy truck? *(Write your answer on the line.)*

_____ inches

½   1   ½   2   ½   3   ½   4   ½   5   ½   6

- -

Measurement and Geometry

DAILY Warm-Up 60

Name _____ Date _____

1. Are the two figures congruent? *(Circle "Yes" or "No.")*

Yes

No

2. Are the two shapes alike or different? *(Circle "Alike" or "Different.")*

Alike   Different

DAILY Warm-Up 61

Name _____ Date _____

1. Circle the letter that names the shape.

A. pentagon   **B.** hexagon   **C.** octagon

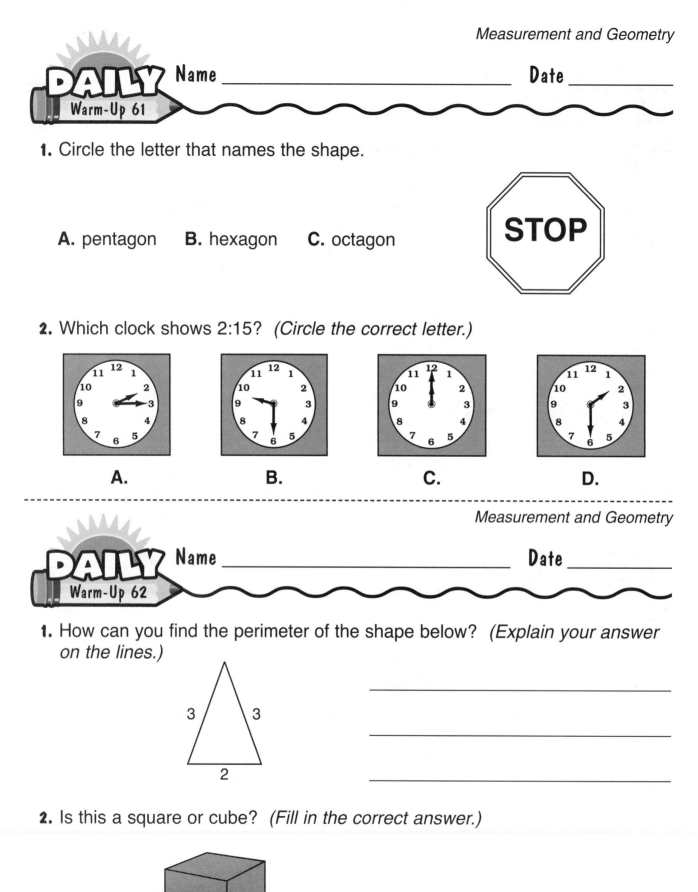

2. Which clock shows 2:15? *(Circle the correct letter.)*

A.   **B.**   **C.**   **D.**

DAILY Warm-Up 62

Name _____ Date _____

1. How can you find the perimeter of the shape below? *(Explain your answer on the lines.)*

3 \ 3

2

_____

_____

_____

2. Is this a square or cube? *(Fill in the correct answer.)*

The shape is a _____ .

Answer Key

Warm-Up 1
1. D
2. 5:05

Warm-Up 2
1. D
2. A

Warm-Up 3
1. 7
2. B

Warm-Up 4
1. C
2. Alike

Warm-Up 5
1. A
2.

Warm-Up 6
1. C
2A. 4:25
2B. 1:30
2C. 2:45
2D. 5:35

Warm-Up 7
1. B
2. B

Warm-Up 8
1. B
2. B

Warm-Up 9
1. 3
2. C

Warm-Up 10
1. 16
2. A = 4, B = 8,
   C = 7

Warm-Up 11
1. C
2. 7, 60

Warm-Up 12
1. C
2. B

Warm-Up 13
1. Yes, No
2. A

Warm-Up 14
1. Answers will vary.
   (Example: One is a solid
   shape and one is a plane
   shape.)
2. C

Warm-Up 15
1. 62
2. 45 minutes

Warm-Up 16
1. C
2. pints

Warm-Up 17
1. Yes
2. True

Warm-Up 18
1. D
2. 4

Warm-Up 19
1. A
2. C

Warm-Up 20
1. B
2. 6

Warm-Up 21
1. C
2. C

Warm-Up 22
1. A
2. 8

Warm-Up 23
1. 28
2. 16

Warm-Up 24
1. A
2. 6

Warm-Up 25
1. 3
2. E, C, D, A

Warm-Up 26
1. May, 31, Thursday
2. 9

Warm-Up 27
1. Yes
2. C

Warm-Up 28
1. 12
2. 9, 11, 4

Warm-Up 29
1. Yes
2. D

Warm-Up 30
1. The one on the right is a
   solid shape and the other is
   a plane shape. Or, the one
   on the right is a sphere and
   the other is a circle.
2. 24

Warm-Up 31
1. B
2.

Warm-Up 32
1. False
2.

3:40	1:30
12:00	3:15

Warm-Up 33
1. Yes
2.

3:45	9:30
5:15	8:20

Answer Key

Warm-Up 34
1. C
2. D

Warm-Up 35
1. False, True
2. C

Warm-Up 36
1. B
2. A

Warm-Up 37
1. Alike
2. A

Warm-Up 38
1. Yes
2. 6, 6

Warm-Up 39
1. B, D, C, A
2. A, B, C, D

Warm-Up 40
1. B
2.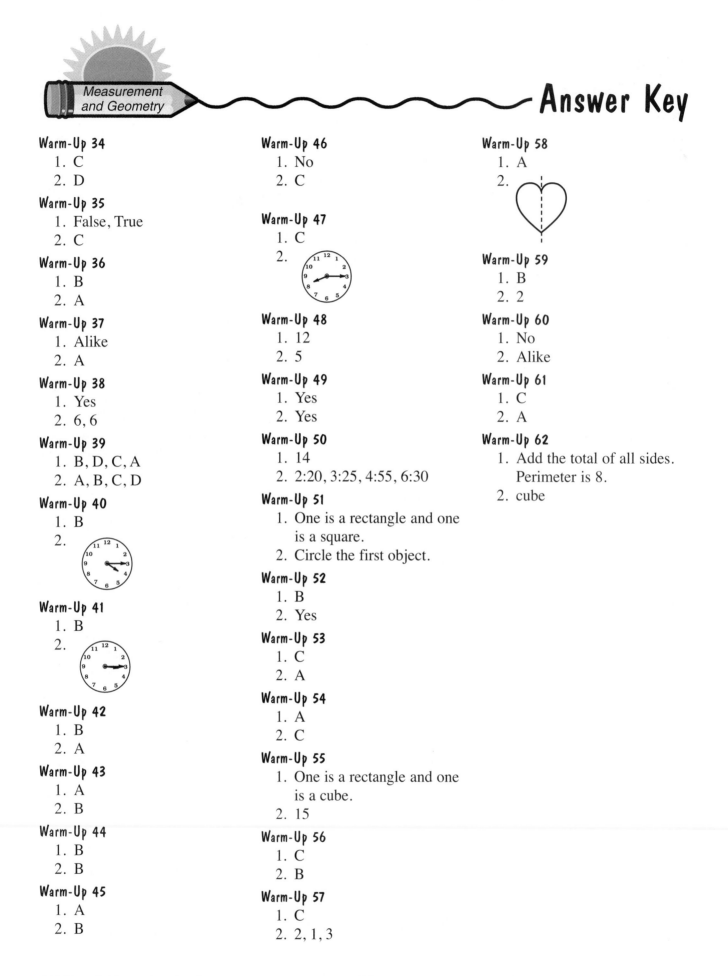

Warm-Up 41
1. B
2.

Warm-Up 42
1. B
2. A

Warm-Up 43
1. A
2. B

Warm-Up 44
1. B
2. B

Warm-Up 45
1. A
2. B

Warm-Up 46
1. No
2. C

Warm-Up 47
1. C
2.

Warm-Up 48
1. 12
2. 5

Warm-Up 49
1. Yes
2. Yes

Warm-Up 50
1. 14
2. 2:20, 3:25, 4:55, 6:30

Warm-Up 51
1. One is a rectangle and one is a square.
2. Circle the first object.

Warm-Up 52
1. B
2. Yes

Warm-Up 53
1. C
2. A

Warm-Up 54
1. A
2. C

Warm-Up 55
1. One is a rectangle and one is a cube.
2. 15

Warm-Up 56
1. C
2. B

Warm-Up 57
1. C
2. 2, 1, 3

Warm-Up 58
1. A
2.

Warm-Up 59
1. B
2. 2

Warm-Up 60
1. No
2. Alike

Warm-Up 61
1. C
2. A

Warm-Up 62
1. Add the total of all sides. Perimeter is 8.
2. cube

GRAPHS, DATA AND PROBABILITY

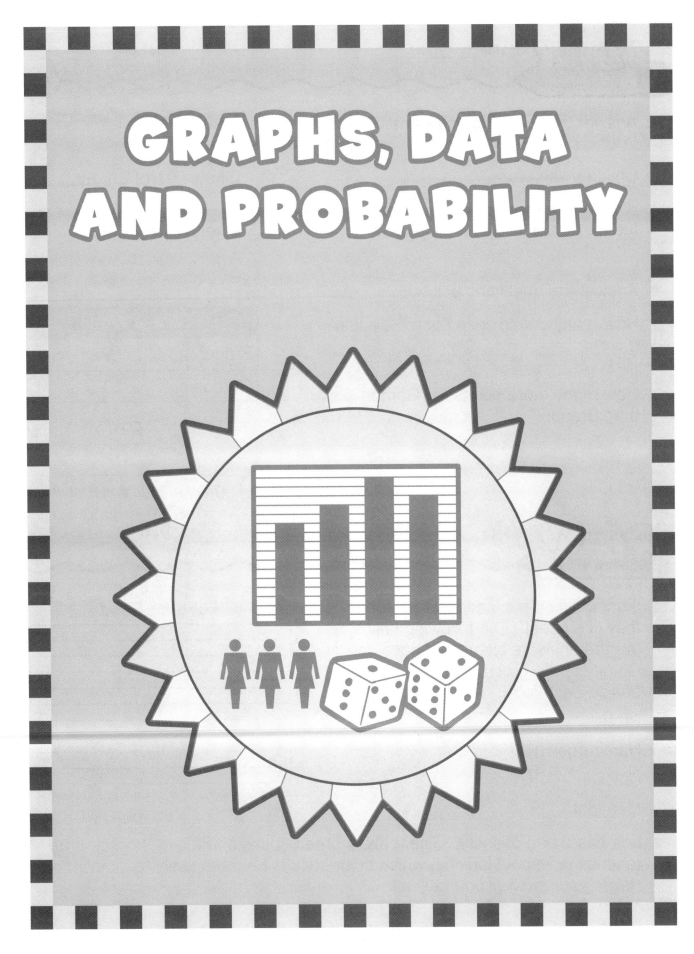

DAILY
Warm-Up 1

Name _____ Date _____

1. Answer the following questions by circling the best answer.

Children like pizza.   **Likely   Not Likely**

Ice melts fast in freezing weather.   **Likely   Not Likely**

2. Answer the questions below.

How many points does each ◯ equal?

_____ points

How many more points did Gordon score than Brandi?

_____ points

Games Won	
Brandi	◯◯◯◯
Gordon	◯◯◯◯◯◯

◯ = 2 points

DAILY
Warm-Up 2

Name _____ Date _____

1. James asked his friends which food they liked best. The following tallies are the answers his friends gave. Complete the graph using the marks beside each food.

Pizza   ⅣⅣ ⅣⅣ

Hamburger   ⅣⅣ ||

Chicken   ⅣⅣ

Meatloaf |

Favorite Food

10
9
8
7
6
5
4
3
2
1
0
Pizza   Hamburger   Chicken   Meatloaf

2. Lee has a bag of socks. There are 4 green socks and 8 blue socks. If he reaches in without looking, which color sock is he more likely to pick? (*Write your answer on the line.*)

_____

Name _____   **Date** _____

1. Circle *true* or *false* for the problem below.

When you toss a coin, it will land on heads or tails.

True   False

2. Use the graph to answer the questions.

How many does each 🥤 equal?

_____

How many shakes did Allie sell?

_____

🥤 = 2 shakes

SHAKES SOLD	
Monica	🥤🥤🥤
Allie	🥤🥤🥤🥤🥤🥤

- -

Name _____   **Date** _____

1. Use the bar graph to answer the questions below.

How many more red marbles
does Hank have than Matt?

_____

Who has the least number of
red marbles?

_____

Red Marbles

Sam
Lou
Matt
Hank

1   2   3   4   5   6   7   8

2. Circle the right answer below.

Tonight, you will have homework.   **Likely**   **Not Likely**

In the summer, it is hot.   **Likely**   **Not Likely**

DAILY Warm-Up 5

Name _____ Date _____

1. Answer the problems below.

Most students eat breakfast before coming to school.   **Likely**   **Not Likely**

People enjoy eating popcorn at the movies.   **Likely**   **Not Likely**

You will find a million dollars on your way to school.   **Likely**   **Not Likely**

2. Use the graph to answer the questions.

How many does each 🖍 equal?

_____

How many crayons does Heather have?

_____

🖍 = 3 crayons

Crayons	
Liz	🖍 🖍 🖍
Heather	🖍 🖍 🖍 🖍

DAILY Warm-Up 6

Name _____ Date _____

1. Use the bar graph to answer the questions below.

Who has the most cards?

_____

Who has the least number of cards?

_____

Card Collection

Jim
Sam
Pat
Rob

1 2 3 4 5 6 7 8

2. Circle the best answer below.

You will read a book this year.   **Likely**   **Not Likely**

You will drive a car home from school.   **Likely**   **Not Likely**

DAILY Warm-Up 7

Name _____ Date _____

1. Circle the answer to the problem below.

You will wear shoes to school.   **Likely**   **Not Likely**

2. Use the graph to answer the questions.

How many does each 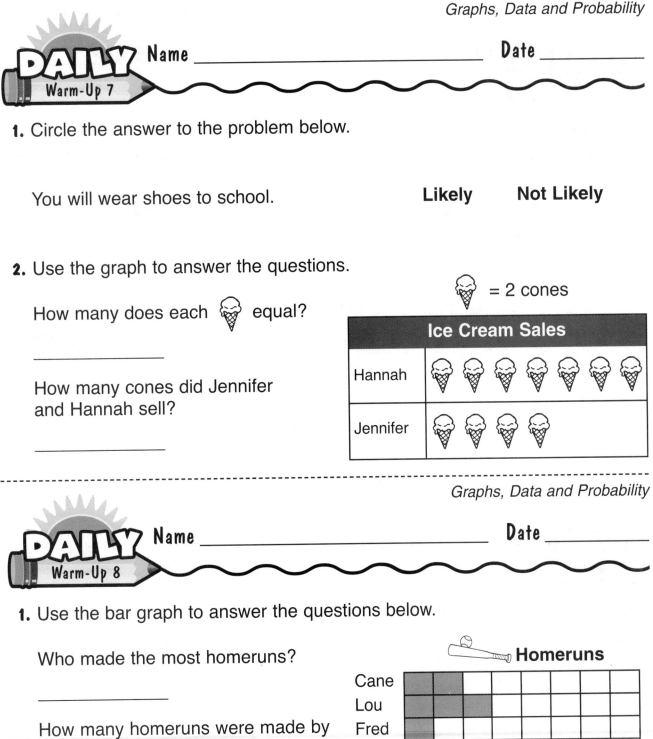 equal?

_____

How many cones did Jennifer and Hannah sell?

_____

= 2 cones

Ice Cream Sales	
Hannah	🍦🍦🍦🍦🍦🍦🍦
Jennifer	🍦🍦🍦🍦

- -

DAILY Warm-Up 8

Name _____ Date _____

1. Use the bar graph to answer the questions below.

Who made the most homeruns?

_____

How many homeruns were made by Cane and Fred combined?

_____

🏏 **Homeruns**

	1	2	3	4	5	6	7	8
Cane								
Lou								
Fred								
Frank								

2. Dave has 3 blue markers and 2 yellow markers in his backpack. If he reaches inside without looking, which color is he likely to pick? (*Write your answer on the line.*)

_____

DAILY Warm-Up 9

Name _____ Date _____

1. Use the bar graph to answer the questions.

How many blue and green candies are there?

_____

How many total colored candies are there?

_____

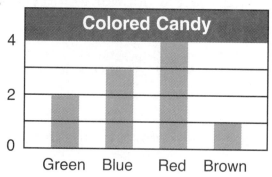

2. Matt and Yolanda are playing a game. On what number do they have the greatest chance of landing? *(Write the answer on the line.)*

_____

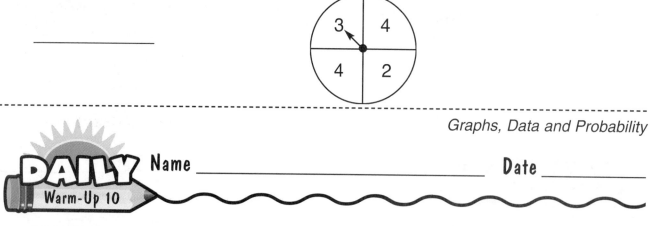

- -

DAILY Warm-Up 10

Name _____ Date _____

1. Use the bar graph to answer the questions below.

Who sold the least number of flags?

_____

How many flags were sold in all?

_____

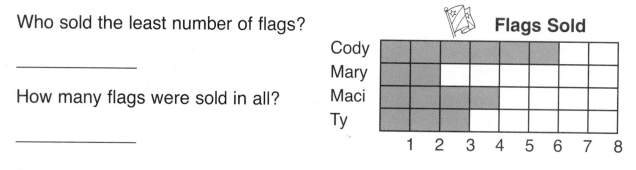

2. Sue has 4 quarters and 3 dimes in her purse. If she reaches in without looking, what coin will she most likely pick? *(Write your answer on the line.)*

_____

DAILY
Warm-Up 11

Name _____   Date _____

1. Answer the following question by circling the best answer.

You will take a bath or shower more than once this week.

Likely   Not Likely

2. Jake has numbered marbles in a jar. If he reaches in, which marble does he have the greatest chance of picking?

_____

Why? _____

_____

_____

DAILY
Warm-Up 12

Name _____   Date _____

1. Use the graph to answer the questions.

How many letters did Cody and Ty receive altogether?

_____

Which two children received an equal amount of letters?

_____

Children Who Received Letters Over the Summer

Sally	✉✉
Ty	✉✉✉✉✉
Cody	✉✉✉
Maci	✉✉✉

✉ = 2 letters

2. On what color will the spinner most likely land? (*Write your answer on the line.*)

_____

blue
blue   black
red

DAILY Name _____ Date _____
Warm-Up 13

1. Which was the favorite food?
(*Circle the correct letter.*)

A. hamburger

B. hot dog

C. pizza

2. Use the graph to answer the questions.
How many people liked basketball
and football more than tennis?

_____

What sport was least liked?

_____

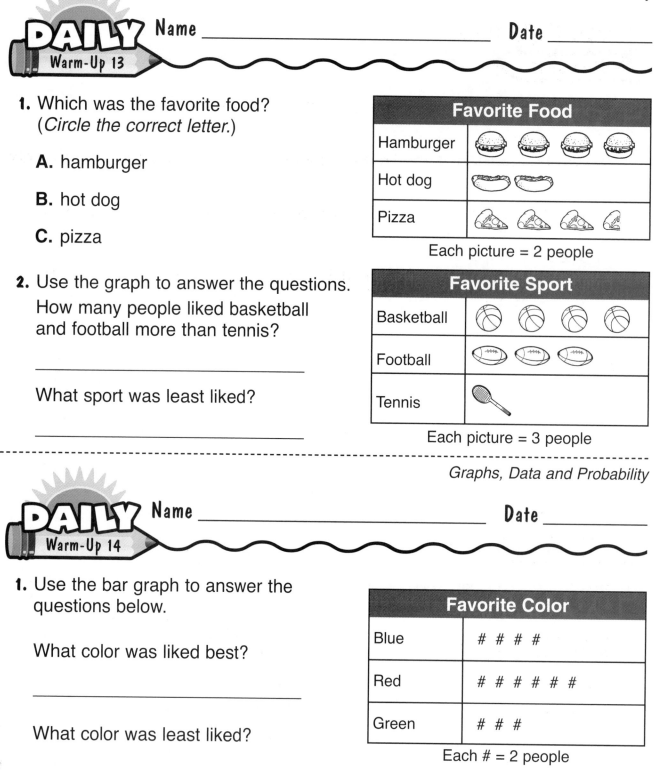

Favorite Food	
Hamburger	
Hot dog	
Pizza	

Each picture = 2 people

Favorite Sport	
Basketball	
Football	
Tennis	

Each picture = 3 people

DAILY Name _____ Date _____
Warm-Up 14

1. Use the bar graph to answer the
questions below.

What color was liked best?

_____

What color was least liked?

_____

Favorite Color	
Blue	# # # #
Red	# # # # # #
Green	# # #

Each # = 2 people

2. Jerry has 3 quarters, 2 dimes, and 1 penny in his pocket. If he grabs one
without looking, what coin will he most likely pick? (*Write your answer on
the line.*)

_____

116

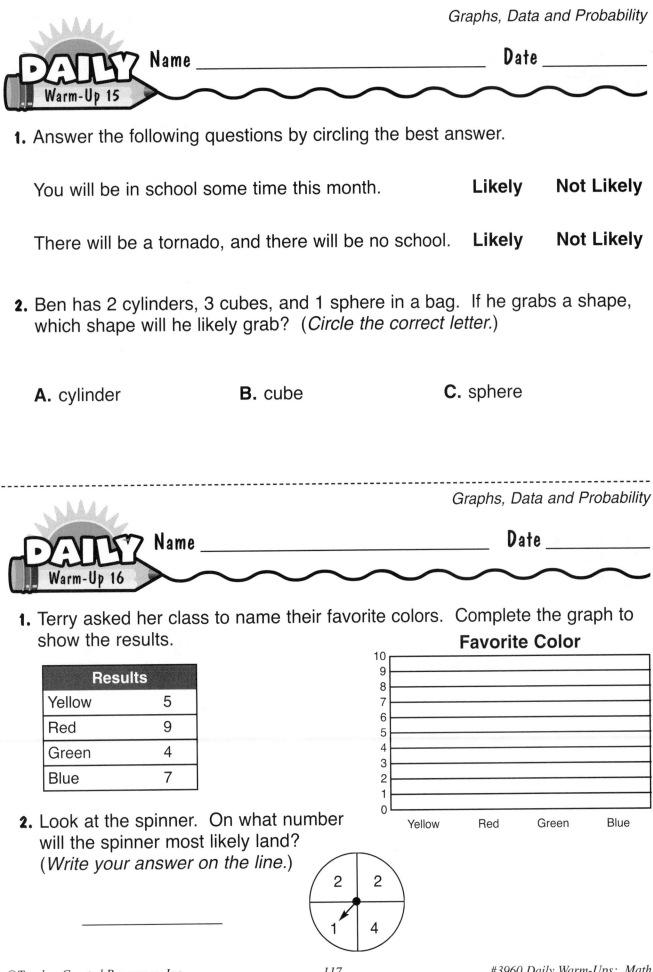

DAILY Warm-Up 15

Name _____ Date _____

1. Answer the following questions by circling the best answer.

You will be in school some time this month. **Likely** **Not Likely**

There will be a tornado, and there will be no school. **Likely** **Not Likely**

2. Ben has 2 cylinders, 3 cubes, and 1 sphere in a bag. If he grabs a shape, which shape will he likely grab? (*Circle the correct letter.*)

A. cylinder **B.** cube **C.** sphere

DAILY Warm-Up 16

Name _____ Date _____

1. Terry asked her class to name their favorite colors. Complete the graph to show the results.

Results	
Yellow	5
Red	9
Green	4
Blue	7

Favorite Color

10
9
8
7
6
5
4
3
2
1
0

Yellow   Red   Green   Blue

2. Look at the spinner. On what number will the spinner most likely land? (*Write your answer on the line.*)

_____

2 2
1 4

DAILY
Warm-Up 17

Name _____ Date _____

1. Circle *likely* or *not likely* for the problems below.

There will be no homework all year.   **Likely**   **Not Likely**

There will be homework tonight.   **Likely**   **Not Likely**

2. Mark the correct answer to the following questions. The first one is done for you.

___**A**___ I will sleep late this weekend.

_____ My teacher will let me teach the class
while she sleeps.

_____ I will drive my teacher's car home after school.

_____ My parents will let me eat candy for supper.

KEY
A. Likely
B. Not Likely

DAILY
Warm-Up 18

Name _____ Date _____

1. Look at the graph. What is one thing you can tell from this graph?

_____

_____

_____

_____

Red Marbles

	1	2	3	4	5	6	7	8
Sam								
Lou								
Matt								
Hank								

2. Janet has 2 blue pens, 1 green pen, and 1 red pen in her backpack. If she grabs 1 pen without looking, which color will she most likely pick? (*Circle the correct letter.*)

A. red   **B.** green   **C.** blue

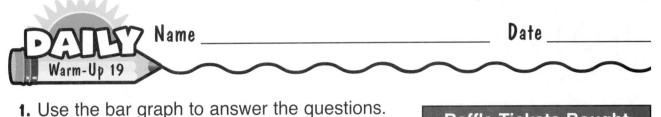

DAILY Name _____ Date _____
Warm-Up 19

1. Use the bar graph to answer the questions.

Which two students bought the most tickets?

_____

How many tickets did Carrie and Mary buy combined?

_____

Raffle Tickets Bought

Carrie Pete Mary Harriet

2. Which spinner has the best chance of landing on a 4? (*Circle the correct letter.*)

A. 3 1 / 4 2

B. 2 4 / 1 3

C. 3 4 / 4 2

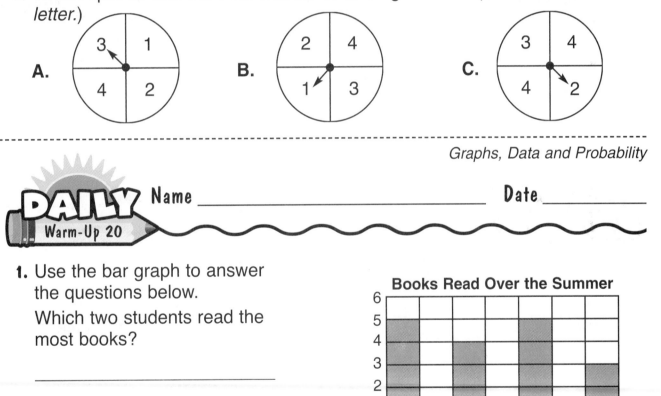

DAILY Name _____ Date _____
Warm-Up 20

1. Use the bar graph to answer the questions below.

Which two students read the most books?

_____

How many books did Terry and Shree read altogether?

_____

Books Read Over the Summer

Cody Terry Robin Shree

2. Orlando has 3 blue beads, 2 yellow beads, and 4 green beads in a jar. If he reaches in, what color will he **least** likely pick? (*Circle the correct letter.*)

A. blue   **B.** yellow   **C.** green

Name _____   Date _____

1. Mr. Rodman drew these shapes on the board. Complete the table about the shapes.

Shape Name	Number of Sides
A.	
B.	
C.	

A.   **B.**   **C.**

2. Roberto has 2 quarters, 3 dimes, and 4 pennies in his pocket. If he reaches in and grabs one, which coin will he **least** likely pick? (*Explain your answer on the lines.*)

_____

_____

_____

- -

DAILY Warm-Up 22

Name _____   Date _____

1. Circle *likely* or *not likely*.

It will rain all week.   **Likely**   **Not Likely**

It will not be hot this summer.   **Likely**   **Not Likely**

2. Circle *true* or *false*.

It is likely you will have homework tonight.   **True**   **False**

It is unlikely you will win a million dollars.   **True**   **False**

It is likely you will start third grade next year.   **True**   **False**

It is unlikely that you will stop growing.   **True**   **False**

DAILY Warm-Up 23

Name _____ Date _____

1. Answer *likely* or *unlikely* to the problems below.

On a freezing cold day, you will wear your swimsuit to school.	**Likely**	**Unlikely**
On a freezing cold day, you will wear warm clothes to school.	**Likely**	**Unlikely**

2. Circle *likely* or *unlikely* to the problems below.

On a hot summer day, you will go swimming.	**Likely**	**Unlikely**
On a hot summer day, you can build a snowman outside.	**Likely**	**Unlikely**

- -

DAILY Warm-Up 24

Name _____ Date _____

1. Answer the questions below.

You will go to college.	**Likely**	**Unlikely**
You will go fishing in a pond and catch a whale.	**Likely**	**Unlikely**

2. Circle *true* or *false*.

It is likely you will pass to third grade.	**True**	**False**
It is unlikely you will get a car for Christmas.	**True**	**False**
It is likely you will grow over the summer.	**True**	**False**
It is unlikely your eyes will change color.	**True**	**False**
It is likely you will make new friends this year.	**True**	**False**

DAILY
Warm-Up 25

Name _____   Date _____

1. Answer *likely* or *not likely*.

Glass breaks if you drop it.   **Likely**   **Not Likely**

You will get an upset stomach if   **Likely**   **Not Likely**
you eat too much candy.

2. Sarah has 3 quarters, 2 dimes, and 6 pennies in her purse. If she reaches in and grabs one, which coin will she **most** likely pick? (*Explain your answer on the lines.*)

_____

_____

_____

DAILY
Warm-Up 26

Name _____   Date _____

1. Use the spinner to answer the problem. (*Circle your answer.*)

You have an even chance of landing
on a shaded region.

True   **False**

2. Use the graph to answer the questions. How many students have no computer in their homes?

_____

How many students have two computers in their homes?

_____

Number of Computers in Students' Homes

0 Computer	1 Computer	2 Computers	3 Computers
	💾		
	💾	💾	
💾	💾	💾	
💾	💾	💾	💾

💾 = 2 students

DAILY
Warm-Up 27

Name _____ Date _____

1. Answer *likely* or *not likely*.

You will play games at school the whole day.　　**Likely**　　**Not Likely**

Your teacher will let you stop doing homework.　　**Likely**　　**Not Likely**

2. Use the bar graph to answer the questions.

How many students liked the color blue?

_____

How many students were asked?

_____

Students' Favorite Color

	1	2	3	4	5
Yellow	▓				
Blue	▓	▓	▓	▓	
Green	▓	▓			
Red	▓	▓	▓	▓	▓

Number of Votes

- -

DAILY
Warm-Up 28

Name _____ Date _____

1. Answer *true* or *false* to the problem below.

It is likely you will learn to ride a bike.　　**True**　　**False**

It is unlikely you will drive a boat to school.　　**True**　　**False**

2. Use the graph to solve the problems.

How many minutes does Carry read each day?

_____ minutes

How many minutes do Carry and Peggy read each day altogether?

_____ minutes

Time Spent Reading

Carry	📖 📖 📖 📖 📖 📖
Cindy	📖 📖 📖 📖
Peggy	📖 📖 📖 📖 📖
Sierra	📖 📖

📖 = 10 minutes reading each day

DAILY Warm-Up 29

Name _____   Date _____

1. Use the information below to complete the graph.

Yellow	4
Blue	5
Red	3
Green	7
Orange	6

Number of Jelly Beans

	1	2	3	4	5	6	7	8
Yellow								
Blue								
Red								
Green								
Orange								

2. Answer *true* or *false*.

It is likely you will learn to swim.   **True**   **False**

It is unlikely you will ever use a computer.   **True**   **False**

DAILY Warm-Up 30

Name _____   Date _____

1. Answer *true* or *false*.

It is unlikely an elephant can take a bath in 1 gallon of water.   **True**   **False**

It is likely a whale can live in 5 gallons of water.   **True**   **False**

2. Use the graph to solve the problems. What color eyes do most students have?

_____

How many students have brown eyes?

_____ students

Student Eye Color

Blue	👁 👁 👁 👁
Brown	👁 👁 👁 👁 👁 👁
Green	👁 👁 👁
Blue/Green	👁 👁

👁 = 2 children

DAILY Warm-Up 31

Name _____ Date _____

1. Use the information to complete the bar graph.

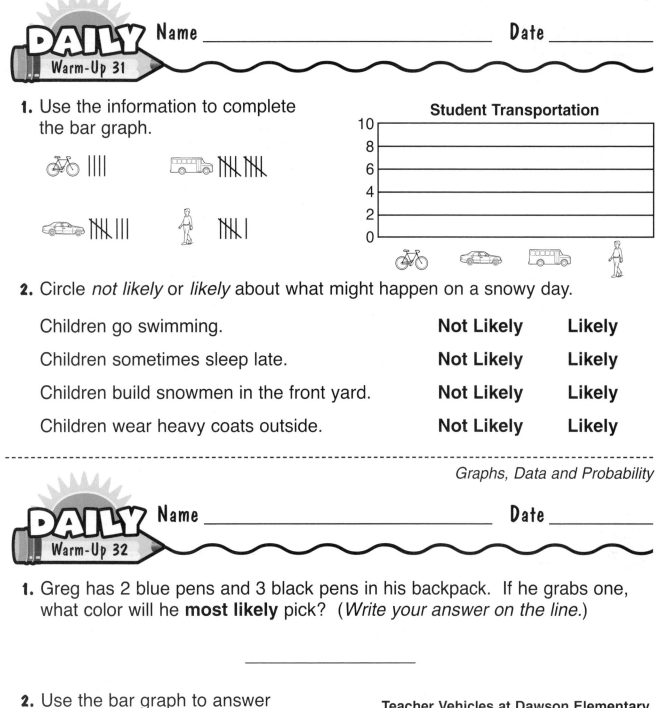

2. Circle *not likely* or *likely* about what might happen on a snowy day.

Children go swimming.	**Not Likely**	**Likely**
Children sometimes sleep late.	**Not Likely**	**Likely**
Children build snowmen in the front yard.	**Not Likely**	**Likely**
Children wear heavy coats outside.	**Not Likely**	**Likely**

DAILY Warm-Up 32

Name _____ Date _____

1. Greg has 2 blue pens and 3 black pens in his backpack. If he grabs one, what color will he **most likely** pick? (*Write your answer on the line.*)

_____

2. Use the bar graph to answer the questions below.

How many teachers drive a van?

_____

Which vehicle do teachers drive most?

_____

How many trucks and cars are owned by teachers at Dawson Elementary?

_____

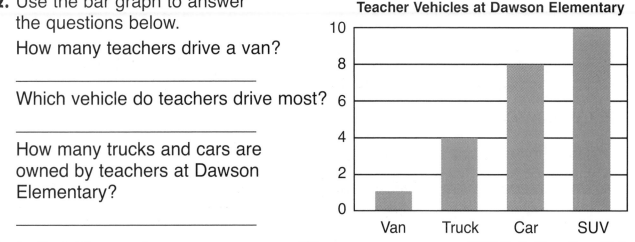

Teacher Vehicles at Dawson Elementary

DAILY Name _____   Date _____
Warm-Up 33

1. Sue has 3 blue buttons, 2 yellow buttons, and 1 orange button in a jar. If she grabs one, which color will she **most likely** pick? (*Circle the correct letter.*)

   A. blue   **B.** yellow   **C.** orange

2. Use the graph to answer the questions.

   How many does each 📞 equal?

   _____

   How many phone calls did Carol make?

   _____

   📞 = 2 phone calls

Crayons	
Carol	📞 📞 📞 📞
Diana	📞 📞 📞

DAILY Name _____   Date _____
Warm-Up 34

1. Use the bar graph to answer the questions below.

   Who won the fewest games?

   _____

   How many games did Mary and Francis win together?

   _____

   Basketball Results

2. Circle *likely* or *not likely.*

   The sun will come up in the morning.   **Likely**   **Not Likely**

   During recess, you will leave and go shopping.   **Likely**   **Not Likely**

DAILY Warm-Up 35

Name _____ Date _____

1. On what number will the spinner most likely land?
(Circle the correct letter.)

A. 1   **B.** 2   **C.** 3   **D.** 4

2. Use the graph to answer the questions.

How many does each ☺ equal?

_____

How many tickets did Wanda sell?

_____

☺ = **10 Tickets Sold**

Wanda	☺ ☺ ☺ ☺ ☺
Maci	☺ ☺ ☺

DAILY Warm-Up 36

Name _____ Date _____

1. Uses the bar graph to answer the questions below.

How many more miles did Sue walk than Sally?

_____

How many miles were walked altogether?

_____

Miles Walked

2. Circle *likely* or *not likely* about what might happen over your time off from school.

You will go on vacation.   **Likely**   **Not Likely**

You will do homework every night of the week.   **Likely**   **Not Likely**

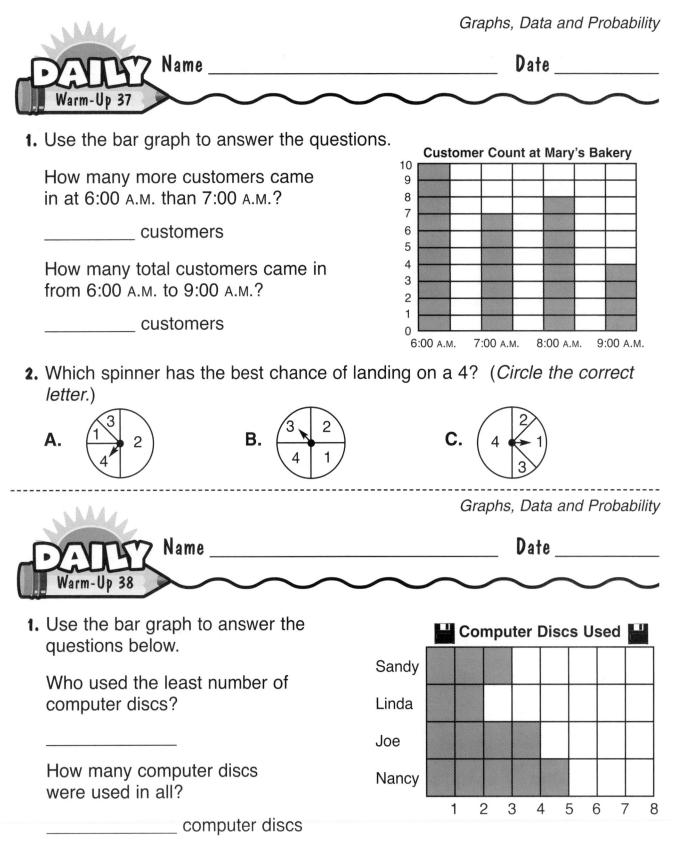

DAILY Warm-Up 37

Name _____ Date _____

1. Use the bar graph to answer the questions.

How many more customers came in at 6:00 A.M. than 7:00 A.M.?

_____ customers

How many total customers came in from 6:00 A.M. to 9:00 A.M.?

_____ customers

Customer Count at Mary's Bakery

2. Which spinner has the best chance of landing on a 4? (*Circle the correct letter.*)

A.

B.

C.

DAILY Warm-Up 38

Name _____ Date _____

1. Use the bar graph to answer the questions below.

Who used the least number of computer discs?

_____

How many computer discs were used in all?

_____ computer discs

Computer Discs Used

2. Gene has 3 red shirts, 2 green shirts, and 1 white shirt in his closet. If he grabs one without looking, what color will he **least** likely pick? (*Circle the correct letter.*)

A. red   **B.** green   **C.** white

DAILY
Warm-Up 39

Name _____ Date _____

1. Circle *likely* or *not likely* for the problems below.

During the summer, it is hot.   **Likely**   **Not Likely**

During the winter, it is cold.   **Likely**   **Not Likely**

2. Mark the correct answer to the following questions. The first one is done for you.

___**B**___ I will never have to do homework.

_____ My teacher will give me his or her car.

_____ I will not make new friends.

_____ I will have cake for my birthday.

KEY
A. Likely
B. Not Likely

DAILY
Warm-Up 40

Name _____ Date _____

1. Look at the graph. Answer the questions.

How many laps did Sam and
Lou run together?

_____ laps

Who ran the most laps? _____

Who ran the least laps? _____

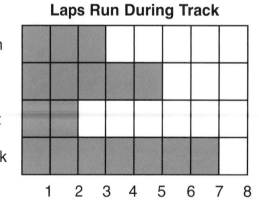

Laps Run During Track

2. Donna has 2 orange crayons, 3 blue crayons, and 1 yellow crayon. If she grabs one, which color will she **most** likely pick? (*Circle the correct letter.*)

A. yellow   **B.** blue   **C.** orange

DAILY Warm-Up 41 · Name _____ Date _____

1. Use the information below to complete the graph. Shade in one square for each vote.

Salvador	6
Issac	8
Tremesha	4
Damon	7
Dave	5

Votes For Most Popular Student

	1	2	3	4	5	6	7	8
Salvador								
Isaac								
Tremesha								
Damon								
Dave								

Number of Votes

2. Circle *likely* or *unlikely*.

You will take a rocket to school. **Likely Unlikely**

You will dig in my backyard and find dinosaur fossils. **Likely Unlikely**

DAILY Warm-Up 42 · Name _____ Date _____

1. Circle *true* or *false*.

You are taller than an adult giraffe. **True False**

You will fly in a car. **True False**

2. Use the graph to solve the problems.

Which color shirt was worn by the most students?

_____

Each 👕 represents _____ children.

How many children wore blue shirts? _____

Color of Shirts

Red	👕 👕 👕 👕 👕
Blue	👕 👕 👕 👕
White	👕 👕 👕
Navy	👕

👕 = 5 children

DAILY Warm-Up 43

Name _____ Date _____

1. Answer the following sentences by circling the right answer.

Tonight, I will have supper with the president.   **Likely   Not Likely**

This summer, I will read two books.   **Likely   Not Likely**

2. On what object will the spinner most likely land?
(*Circle the correct letter.*)

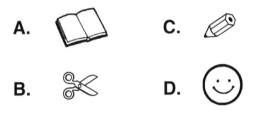
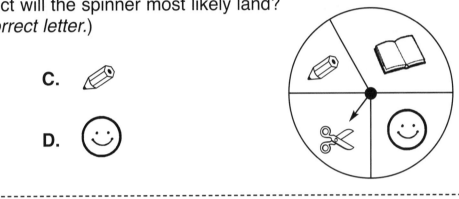

A. ▱   **C.** ✏

B. ✂   **D.** ☺

DAILY Warm-Up 44

Name _____ Date _____

1. Terry asked her class what to name their favorite ice cream. Complete the graph by showing the results.

RESULTS	
Strawberry	2
Vanilla	7
Chocolate	10
Swirl	4

Favorite Ice Cream

10
9
8
7
6
5
4
3
2
1
0

Chocolate   Swirl   Vanilla   Strawberry

2. Circle *true* or *false*.

Brushing your teeth will give you cavities.   **True   False**

Studying will make you smarter.   **True   False**

DAILY Warm-Up 45

Name _____ Date _____

1. Circle *true* or *false* for the statements below.

It is unlikely you will take a bath or shower this week.　　　**True**　　**False**

Hurricanes cause damage.　　　**True**　　**False**

My teacher will get upset if I do not do my homework.　　　**True**　　**False**

2. Mary Lou has a bag of letters. If she grabs one letter without looking, what letter will she **most** likely pick?

She will most likely pick the letter _____.

Why? _____

_____

_____

J　G
B　M　J
A　K　J

DAILY Warm-Up 46

Name _____ Date _____

1. Use the graph to answer the questions.

Movies Watched Over the Summer

Jed	🎥 🎥 🎥 🎥
Mike	🎥 🎥 🎥
Liz	🎥 🎥 🎥 🎥 🎥
Betty	🎥 🎥

🎥 = 3 movies

How many movies did Jed and Liz watch altogether?

_____

How many movies more did Liz watch than Betty?

_____

2. If Mrs. Brown hit the spinner, on what color will it most likely land? *(Write your answer on the line.)*

_____

yellow
yellow　yellow
green

DAILY Warm-Up 47

Name _____ Date _____

1. How many students picked skating as their favorite field trip?

A. 9   **B.** 12   **C.** 24

Votes for Favorite Field Trip	
Movies	|||| |||| ||
Skating	|||| |||| |||| |||| ||||
Zoo	|||| ||||

2. Use the graph to answer the questions.

How many points were scored by Jerry and Cindy altogether?

_____ points

How many points did Margaret score?

_____ points

Number of Basketball Points	
Jerry	◯ ◯
Cindy	◯ ◯ ◯ ◯
Margaret	◯ ◯ ◯ ◯ ◯ ◯

◯ = 2 points

DAILY Warm-Up 48

Name _____ Date _____

1. Use the graph to answer the questions below.

How many points did the blue team score?

_____

Which team scored the least points?

_____

Which team scored the most points?

_____

Each 🧍 = 3 points

Team Points	
Blue	🧍 🧍 🧍 🧍 🧍
Red	🧍 🧍 🧍
Green	🧍 🧍 🧍 🧍 🧍 🧍 🧍

2. Answer *true* or *false*.

If you flip a coin, you will always get heads or tails.   **True**   **False**

It is unlikely your dog can do your homework.   **True**   **False**

DAILY
Warm-Up 49

Name _____ Date _____

1. Circle the correct answer to the problems.

It is likely a paper airplane could fly 20 miles.   **Likely**   **Not Likely**

After school today, you will fly to Europe.   **Likely**   **Not Likely**

You will vacation in Africa and catch a lion.   **Likely**   **Not Likely**

2. Use the graph to answer the questions.

= 4 birds

How many does each 🐦 equal?

_____

How many birds did Tammy see?

_____

Birds in a Field	
Jimmy	🐦🐦🐦🐦🐦
Tammy	🐦🐦🐦🐦

DAILY
Warm-Up 50

Name _____ Date _____

1. Use the bar graph to answer the questions below.

How many trophies did David win?

_____

Who won the fewest trophies?

_____

Each 🏆 = 2 trophies

Trophies Earned	
David	🏆🏆🏆🏆
Kerry	🏆🏆🏆🏆🏆🏆
Jody	🏆🏆🏆🏆🏆

2. Circle the right answer below.

You will run 20 miles each day for a week.   **Likely**   **Not Likely**

Your teacher will give each student $20.   **Likely**   **Not Likely**

DAILY
Warm-Up 51

Name _____

Date _____

1. Circle *true* or *false* for the problem below.

It is likely the shape below can be folded along the lines to form a sphere.

True   False

2. Use the graph to answer the questions.

How many does each ✍ equal?

= 3 letters written

_____

How many letters did Maria and Abby write together?

_____

Letters Written	
Maria	✍ ✍ ✍
Abby	✍ ✍ ✍ ✍

DAILY
Warm-Up 52

Name _____

Date _____

1. Use the bar graph to answer the questions below.

How many pencils and pens does Jake have?

_____

How many more crayons than pens does Jake have?

_____

Jake's Writing Materials

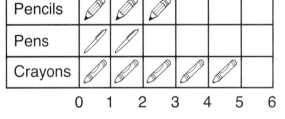

2. Circle the right answer below.

Tonight, you will watch television in a treehouse.   **Likely Not Likely**

Tonight, you will find a whale swimming in your bathtub. **Likely Not Likely**

Tomorrow, you will run for governor of Texas.   **Likely Not Likely**

DAILY
Warm-Up 53

Name _____ Date _____

1. Circle *true* or *false* for the problems below.

It is unlikely you will exercise in P.E. today.   **True**   **False**

It is likely you will have to read in school today.   **True**   **False**

It is likely a dinosaur will enroll at your school.   **True**   **False**

It is unlikely you will ever visit a zoo.   **True**   **False**

2. Use the graph to answer the questions.

How many does each 🎁 equal?

= 3 presents

_____

How many more presents did
Kathy receive than Alexis?

Birthday Presents	
Kathy	🎁 🎁 🎁 🎁
Alexis	🎁 🎁

_____

DAILY
Warm-Up 54

Name _____ Date _____

1. What is one thing this graph tells you?

_____

_____

_____

_____

Homeruns

	1	2	3	4	5	6	7	8
Cane	■	■						
Lou	■	■	■					
Fred	■							
Frank	■							

2. Answer the problems below by circling the correct answer.

This summer will be hot.   **Likely**   **Unlikely**

Today, you will ride a cow home from school.   **Likely**   **Unlikely**

Today, you will laugh at a friend's joke.   **Likely**   **Unlikely**

DAILY
Warm-Up 55

Name _____   Date _____

1. Answer the following problems by circling the right answer.

A wild lion will eat your lunch.	**Likely**	**Not Likely**
You will train a dog to do your math homework.	**Likely**	**Not Likely**
You will go to a friend's house this week.	**Likely**	**Not Likely**
Your teacher will come to your house and mow your lawn.	**Likely**	**Not Likely**

2. Peter has 2 red shirts, 4 blue shirts, and 1 green shirt hanging in his closet. If he grabs one without looking, which color shirt will he **least** likely pick? (*Circle the correct letter.*)

A. red   **B.** blue   **C.** green

DAILY
Warm-Up 56

Name _____   Date _____

1. The graph shows the number of laps Robin swam during a 4-day period. Use the information below to complete the graph.

Monday	7
Tuesday	4
Wednesday	9
Thursday	5

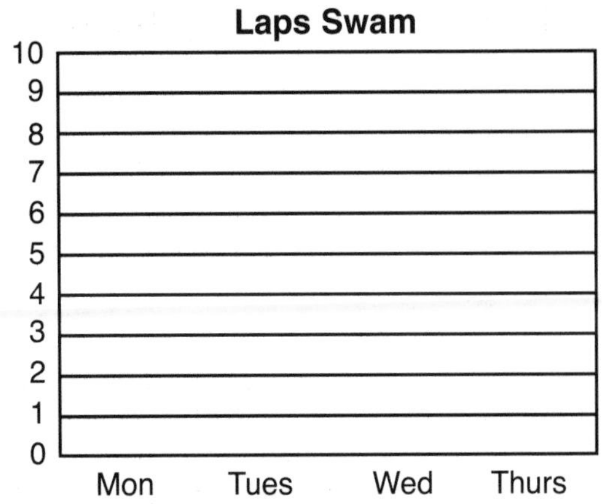

Laps Swam

2. Look at the spinner. On what number will the spinner most likely land? (*Write your answer on the line.*)

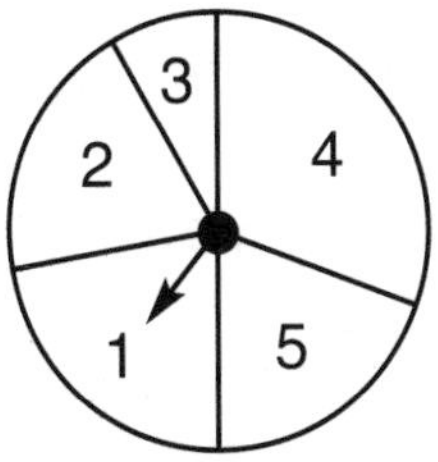

_____

DAILY Warm-Up 57

Name _____ Date _____

1. Answer the problems below.

Which snack was most liked?

_____

How many more students chose apples than oranges as their favorite snack?

_____

Class Favorite Snack	
Apple	1 1 1 1 1 1
Banana	1 1 1
Orange	1 1

2. Use your pencil to shade in one box for each ribbon Jed won at Field Day.

1st place	|||
2nd place	||
3rd place	⧄⧄⧄

Ribbons Jed Won at Field Day					
1st place					
2nd place					
3rd place					

DAILY Warm-Up 58

Name _____ Date _____

1. What is one thing this graph tells you?

_____

_____

_____

Class Transportation	
Bus	🚌🚌🚌🚌🚌🚌
Car	🚗🚗🚗🚗🚗
Bike	🚲🚲🚲

Each picture = 2 students

2. Circle the best answer.

Today you will play a video game on Mars.   **Likely**   **Not Likely**

Tomorrow you will eat fruit.   **Likely**   **Not Likely**

Next week you will fly to New York.   **Likely**   **Not Likely**

DAILY
Warm-Up 59

Name _____   Date _____

1. On what number will the spinner **least** likely land?

   A. 1   **C.** 3

   B. 2   **D.** 4

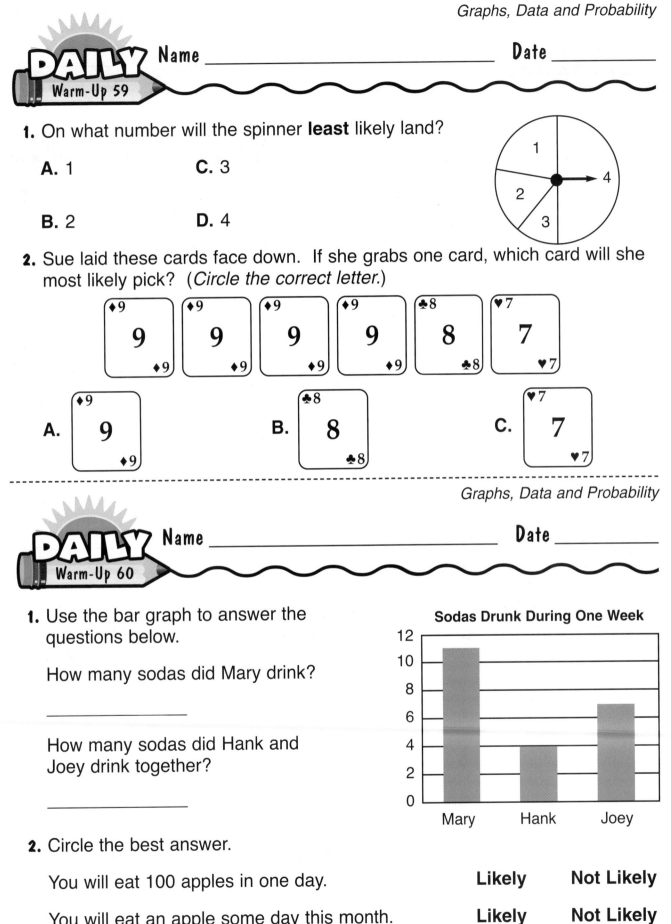

2. Sue laid these cards face down. If she grabs one card, which card will she most likely pick? (*Circle the correct letter.*)

A. 9   **B.** 8   **C.** 7

DAILY
Warm-Up 60

Name _____   Date _____

1. Use the bar graph to answer the questions below.

How many sodas did Mary drink?

_____

How many sodas did Hank and Joey drink together?

_____

Sodas Drunk During One Week

2. Circle the best answer.

You will eat 100 apples in one day.   **Likely**   **Not Likely**

You will eat an apple some day this month.   **Likely**   **Not Likely**

DAILY Warm-Up 61

Name _____ Date _____

1. Use the information to complete the bar graph.

⚽ |||| 🏀 卌 卌

⚾ 卌 ||| 🏑 卌 |

Students' Favorite Sport

```
10
 8
 6
 4
 2
 0
    🏀    ⚾    ⚽    🏑
```

2. Circle *not likely* or *likely* about what might happen on a summer day.

Children go swimming.	**Not Likely**	**Likely**
Some children sleep late.	**Not Likely**	**Likely**
Children build snowmen in the front yard.	**Not Likely**	**Likely**
Children wear heavy coats outside.	**Not Likely**	**Likely**

DAILY Warm-Up 62

Name _____ Date _____

1. George has 3 green ink pens, 2 red ink pens, and 1 black ink pen in his pocket. If he grabs one without looking, what color ink pen will he most likely **not** pick? (*Circle the correct letter.*)

A. green   **B.** red   **C.** black

2. Use the graph to solve the problems below.

Which flower was planted most?

_____

Flowers Planted

Rose	🌸 🌸 🌸 🌸 🌸
Lily	🌸 🌸 🌸
Tulip	🌸 🌸 🌸 🌸

🌸 = 4 flowers

Each 🌸 equal _____ flowers.

How many tulips were planted? _____

Answer Key

Warm-Up 1
1. Likely, Not Likely
2. 2, 4

Warm-Up 2
1.
2. blue

Warm-Up 3
1. True
2. 2 shakes, 12 shakes

Warm-Up 4
1. 5 marbles, Matt
2. Likely, Likely

Warm-Up 5
1. Likely, Likely, Not Likely
2. 3 crayons, 12 crayons

Warm-Up 6
1. Rob, Pat
2. Likely, Not Likely

Warm-Up 7
1. Likely
2. 2 cones, 22 cones

Warm-Up 8
1. Lou, 3 homeruns
2. blue

Warm-Up 9
1. 5 blue and green candies, 10 total
2. 4

Warm-Up 10
1. Mary, 15 flags
2. quarter

Warm-Up 11
1. Likely
2. 10, because there are more of them

Warm-Up 12
1. 20 letters, Cody and Maci
2. blue

Warm-Up 13
1. A
2. 18 people, tennis

Warm-Up 14
1. red, green
2. quarter

Warm-Up 15
1. Likely, Not Likely
2. B

Warm-Up 16
1.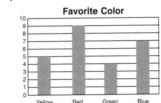
2. 2

Warm-Up 17
1. Not Likely, Likely
2. A, B, B, B

Warm-Up 18
1. Answers will vary.
2. C

Warm-Up 19
1. Pete and Mary, 6 tickets
2. C

Warm-Up 20
1. Cody and Robin, 7 books
2. B

Warm-Up 21
1A. hexagon, 6
1B. pentagon, 5
1C. octagon, 8
2. He will least likely pick a quarter. There are fewer quarters than other coins.

Warm-Up 22
1. Not Likely, Not Likely
2. True, True, True, True

Warm-Up 23
1. Unlikely, Likely
2. Likely, Unlikely

Warm-Up 24
1. Likely, Unlikely
2. True, True, True, True, True

Warm-Up 25
1. Likely, Likely
2. She will most likely pick a penny because there are more pennies (6).

Warm-Up 26
1. True
2. 4 students, 6 students

Warm-Up 27
1. Not Likely, Not Likely
2. 4 students, 12 students

Warm-Up 28
1. True, True
2. 60, 105

Warm-Up 29
1.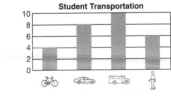
2. True, False

Warm-Up 30
1. True, False
2. brown, 12

Warm-Up 31
1.
2. Not Likely, Likely, Likely, Likely

Warm-Up 32
1. black
2. 1 teacher, SUV, 12 trucks and cars

Warm-Up 33
1. A
2. 2 phone calls, 8 phone calls

Answer Key

Warm-Up 34
1. Francis, 8 games
2. Likely, Not Likely

Warm-Up 35
1. D
2. 10 tickets sold, 45 tickets

Warm-Up 36
1. 3 more miles, 21 miles
2. Likely, Not Likely

Warm-Up 37
1. 3, 29
2. C

Warm-Up 38
1. Linda, 14
2. C

Warm-Up 39
1. Likely, Likely
2. B, B, B, A

Warm-Up 40
1. 8, Hank, Matt
2. B

Warm-Up 41
1.

Votes For Most Popular Student

	1	2	3	4	5	6	7	8
Salvador								
Isaac								
Tremesha								
Damon								
Dave								

Number of Votes

2. Unlikely, Unlikely

Warm-Up 42
1. False, False
2. red, 5, 20

Warm-Up 43
1. Not Likely, Likely
2. A

Warm-Up 44
1.

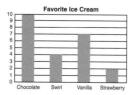

Favorite Ice Cream

2. False, True

Warm-Up 45
1. False, True, True
2. J, because there are more of them

Warm-Up 46
1. 27 movies, 9 movies
2. yellow

Warm-Up 47
1. C
2. 12, 12

Warm-Up 48
1. 15, red, green
2. True, True

Warm-Up 49
1. Not Likely, Not Likely, Not Likely
2. 4 birds, 16 birds

Warm-Up 50
1. 8 trophies, David
2. Not Likely, Not Likely

Warm-Up 51
1. False
2. 3 letters written, 21

Warm-Up 52
1. 5 pencils and pens, 3 more crayons
2. Not Likely, Not Likely, Not Likely

Warm-Up 53
1. False, True, False, False
2. 3 presents, 6 more presents

Warm-Up 54
1. Answers will vary.
2. Likely, Unlikely, Likely

Warm-Up 55
1. Not Likely, Not Likely, Likely, Not Likely
2. C

Warm-Up 56
1.

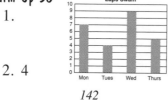

Laps Swam

2. 4

Warm-Up 57
1. apple, 4 more students
2.

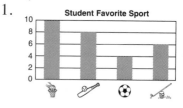

Ribbons Jed Won at Field Day						
1st place						
2nd place						
3rd place						

Warm-Up 58
1. Answers will vary.
2. Not Likely, Likely, Not Likely

Warm-Up 59
1. C
2. A

Warm-Up 60
1. 11 sodas, 11 sodas
2. Not Likely, Likely

Warm-Up 61
1.

Student Favorite Sport

2. Likely, Likely, Not Likely, Not Likely

Warm-Up 62
1. C
2. rose, 4, 16 tulips

ALGEBRA, PATTERNS AND FUNCTIONS

Name _____ **Date** _____

1. Fill in the missing numbers in the pattern below.

56, _____, _____, 59, 60, 61, _____, 63

2. Fill in the next three numbers in the pattern.

Pattern

1st	2nd	3rd	4th	5th	6th
4	6	8			

- -

Name _____ **Date** _____

1. Describe what is happening in the pattern below.

_____

_____

_____

_____

2. Continue the pattern of numbers in the boxes below.

24	22	20		16		10

Name _____ **Date** _____

1. Fill in the missing numbers in the pattern below.

4, 8, 12, 16, _____, _____, _____

2. Beth wrote a pattern of numbers on the board. Fill in the numbers missing in her pattern.

Beth's Pattern

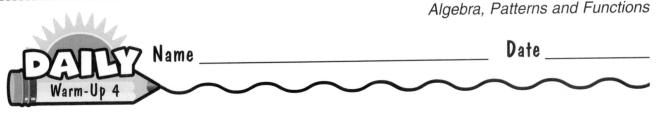

5	10	15	20	25	30
	40	45	50		60
65		75	80		

Name _____ **Date** _____

1. Continue the pattern below.

11, 13, 15, _____ , _____ , _____ , _____, 25

2. Continue the pattern of numbers in the boxes below.

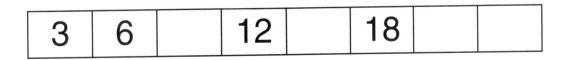

3	6	12	18		

DAILY Warm-Up 5

Name _____   Date _____

1. Look at the number pattern below. Fill in the numbers that go in the empty boxes.

		20	22	24	26

2. Which pattern below is like the pattern in the box? (*Circle the correct letter.*)

Red,	Red,	Blue,	Red,	Red,	Blue

   A. Blue, Blue, Green, Green, Blue, Blue

   B. Yellow, Yellow, Orange, Yellow, Yellow, Orange

   C. Pink, Green, Purple, Pink, Green, Purple

DAILY Warm-Up 6

Name _____   Date _____

1. Look at the table. If 6 is put in the "IN" column, what would be the number in the "OUT" column? (*Write the number in the box.*)

IN	OUT
2	6
4	12
6	

2. Continue the pattern of numbers in the boxes below.

1	3		7		11	13	

DAILY Warm-Up 7

Name _____ **Date** _____

1. Solve the problem below.

$$24 - 10 = 14 \qquad \text{so} \qquad 24 - 14 = \boxed{}$$

2. Solve the problem below.

$$3 + \boxed{} = 6 + 2$$

DAILY Warm-Up 8

Name _____ **Date** _____

1. Find the pattern to fill in the missing number.

IN	1	2	3	4	5	6
OUT	0	1	2	3	4	

2. Continue the pattern of numbers in the boxes below.

2		6		10	12	14	

DAILY Warm-Up 9   Name _____   Date _____

1. Draw the missing shape in the pattern below.

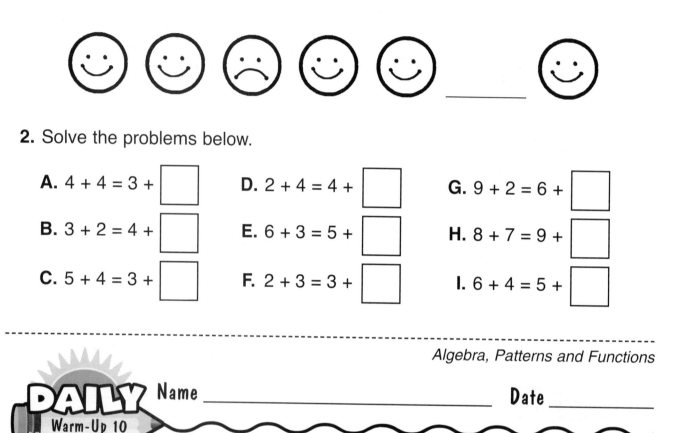

2. Solve the problems below.

A. 4 + 4 = 3 + ☐   **D.** 2 + 4 = 4 + ☐   **G.** 9 + 2 = 6 + ☐

B. 3 + 2 = 4 + ☐   **E.** 6 + 3 = 5 + ☐   **H.** 8 + 7 = 9 + ☐

C. 5 + 4 = 3 + ☐   **F.** 2 + 3 = 3 + ☐   **I.** 6 + 4 = 5 + ☐

DAILY Warm-Up 10   Name _____   Date _____

1. Look at the table below.

IN	1	2	3	4	5	6
OUT	2	4	6	8	10	12

What is being done to the "IN" numbers to get the "OUT" numbers?

_____

_____

2. Fill in the boxes and answer the problems below.

IN	1	2	3	4	5	6
OUT	0	1	2	3		

What is the rule?

_____

IN	0	1	2	3	4	5
OUT	2	3	4	5		

What is the rule?

_____

DAILY Warm-Up 11   Name _____   Date _____

1. Draw the missing shape in the pattern below.

2. Solve the problems below.

A. 2 + 3 = 3 + ☐   **D.** 4 + 4 = 5 + ☐   **G.** 3 + 2 = 1 + ☐

B. 5 + 2 = 4 + ☐   **E.** 7 + 3 = 5 + ☐   **H.** 2 + 7 = 8 + ☐

C. 5 + 1 = 4 + ☐   **F.** 6 + 3 = 3 + ☐   **I.** 3 + 4 = 5 + ☐

DAILY Warm-Up 12   Name _____   Date _____

1. Look at the table below.

IN	11	10	9	8	7	6
OUT	6	5	4	3	2	1

What is being done to the "IN" numbers to get the "OUT" numbers?

_____

_____

2. Answer the problems below.

IN	2	3	4	5	6	7
OUT	4	5	6	7	8	9

What is the rule?

_____

IN	9	8	7	6	5	4
OUT	6	5	4	3	2	1

What is the rule?

_____

DAILY Warm-Up 13

Name _____ Date _____

1. Look at the pattern of numbers. Write what comes next in the pattern.

2, 6, 10, _____ , _____

2. Look at the pattern. Draw the missing two shapes.

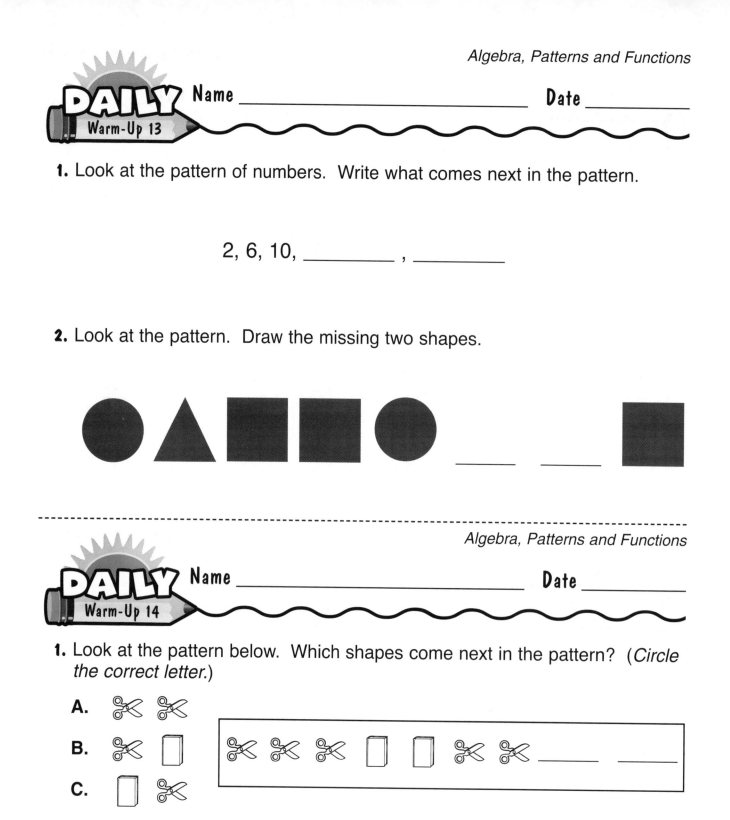

DAILY Warm-Up 14

Name _____ Date _____

1. Look at the pattern below. Which shapes come next in the pattern? (*Circle the correct letter.*)

A.

B.

C.

2. Solve the problem.

$9 + w = 15$

$w =$ _____

Name _____ **Date** _____

Warm-Up 15

1. On Monday, Sally earned $2 selling lemonade. On Tuesday, she earned $4, and on Wednesday, she earned $6. If this pattern continues, how much money will she earn on Thursday? (*Fill in the box.*)

Lemonade	
Monday	$2
Tuesday	$4
Wednesday	$6
Thursday	

2. What comes next in the pattern? (*Circle the correct letter.*)

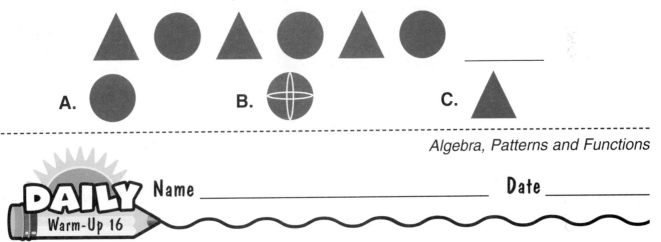

A.   B.   C.

- -

Name _____ **Date** _____

Warm-Up 16

1. Look at the pattern below. Which numbers come next in the pattern? (*Circle the correct letter.*)

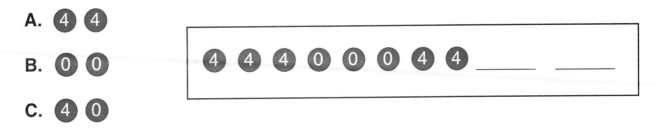

A. 4 4

B. 0 0

C. 4 0

4 4 4 0 0 0 4 4 ____ ____

2. Solve the problem.

$$12 + y = 45$$

$$y = \underline{\quad}$$

DAILY Warm-Up 17

Name _____ Date _____

1. Solve the problem.

$$3 + 5 = 2 + \boxed{}$$

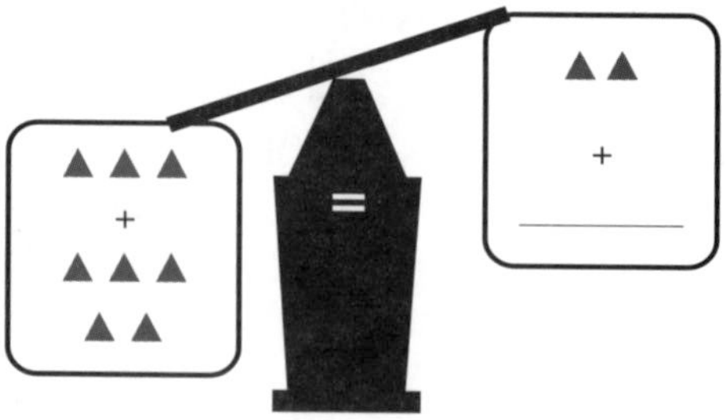

What missing number will balance the scale?

2. Solve the problem.

$$\boxed{} + 4 = 9 + 5$$

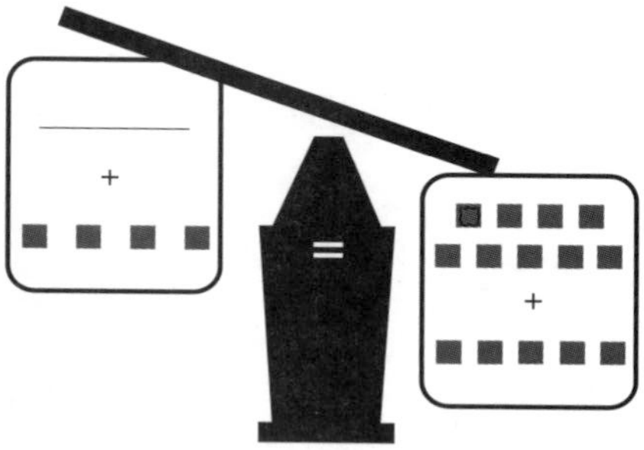

What missing number will balance the scale?

DAILY Warm-Up 18

Name _____ Date _____

1. Solve the problem.

$$4 + 13 = \boxed{} + 7$$

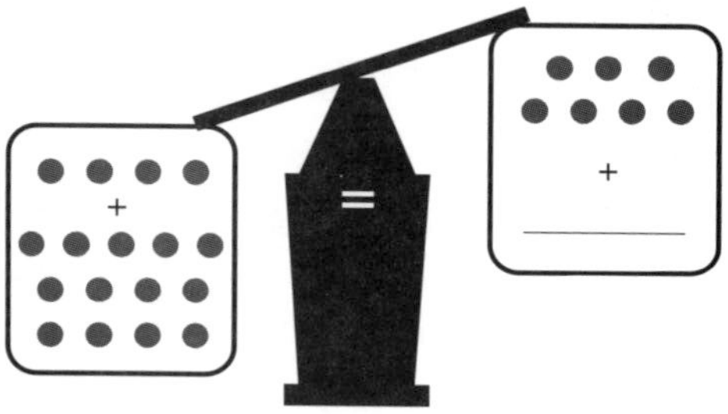

What missing number will balance the scale?

2. What is missing in the pattern? (*Circle the correct letter.*)

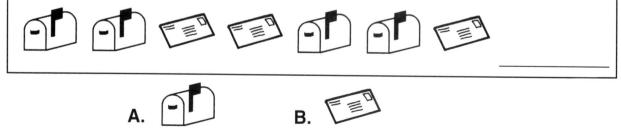

A. **B.**

Name _____   **Date** _____

1. Fill in the missing number in the pattern below.

13, 14, 15, 16, 17, 18, _____ , 20

2. The table shows the number of cookies Mike ate during a cookie-eating contest. If this pattern continues, how many cookies would Mike eat after 5 minutes? (*Fill in the box.*)

Cookie-Eating Contest

Minutes	1	2	3	4	5
Cookies	3	6	9	12	

Name _____   **Date** _____

1. Jim walked 2 miles on Monday, 4 miles on Tuesday, and 6 miles on Wednesday. If he continues his pattern, how many miles will he walk on Thursday? (*Write your answer on the line.*)

_____ miles

2. Find the missing number in the pattern.

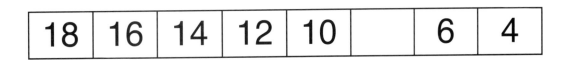

18	16	14	12	10		6	4

DAILY Warm-Up 21   **Name** _____   **Date** _____

1. Using the numbers 0, 2, 3, 5, 6, and 8, make each line add up to 12 (down, across, and corner to corner). (*The first is done for you.*)

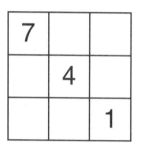

7		
	4	
		1

2. Copy on the blank domino the numbers that will complete the pattern.

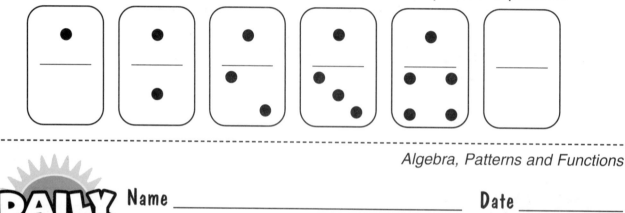

- -

DAILY Warm-Up 22   **Name** _____   **Date** _____

1. Fill in the number that is missing in the pattern.

12,   14,   _____,   18,   20

2. Continue the pattern.

1, 1, 2, 2, 3, 3, 4, 4, 5, 5, 6, _____

DAILY
Warm-Up 23

Name _____   Date _____

1. Fill in the numbers that come next in the pattern.

1, 1, 1, 2, 2, 3, 3, 3, 4, 4, 5, ____, ____

2. What is being done to the "IN" numbers to get the "OUT" numbers?

IN	11	10	9	8	7	6
OUT	6	5	4	3	2	1

_____

_____

_____

- -

DAILY
Warm-Up 24

Name _____   Date _____

1. Fill in the missing numbers to show equal values.

$$3 + \underline{\quad} = 4 + 5$$

$$2 + 5 = 6 + \underline{\quad}$$

2. Circle *True* or *False* for the problems below.

$$5 + \boxed{7} = 6 + 6 \qquad\qquad \textbf{True} \qquad \textbf{False}$$

$$10 + \boxed{5} = 8 + 8 \qquad\qquad \textbf{True} \qquad \textbf{False}$$

DAILY Warm-Up 25

Name _____ Date _____

1. What shape goes in the empty space? (*Circle the correct letter.*)

A.

B.

C.

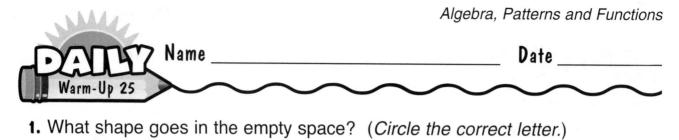

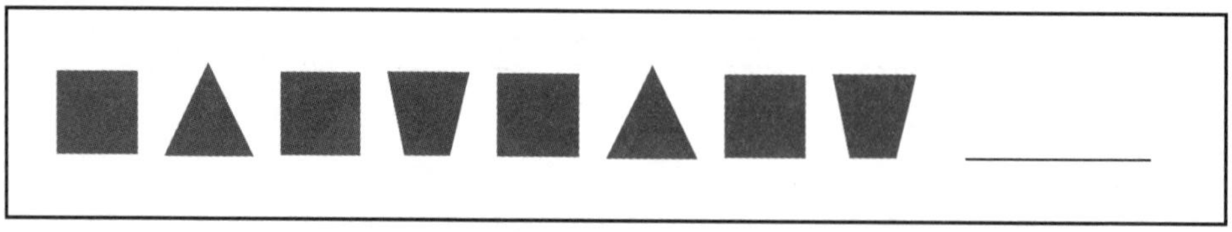

2. Fill in the missing number that makes the problem true.

$$5 + 2 = 3 + \underline{\quad}$$

DAILY Warm-Up 26

Name _____ Date _____

1. Fill in the missing number that makes the problem true.

$$12 + \underline{\quad} = 9 + 9$$

2. Fill in the missing number in the pattern below.

IN	2	3	4	5
OUT	5	6	7	

DAILY Warm-Up 27

Name _____ **Date** _____

1. Look at the pattern of shaded numbers on the hundred chart. Explain what is being done.

_____

_____

_____

1	2	3	4	5	6	7	8	9	10
11	12	13	14	15	16	17	18	19	20
21	22	23	24	25	26	27	28	29	30
31	32	33	34	35	36	37	38	39	40
41	42	43	44	45	46	47	48	49	50
51	52	53	54	55	56	57	58	59	60
61	62	63	64	65	66	67	68	69	70
71	72	73	74	75	76	77	78	79	80
81	82	83	84	85	86	87	88	89	90
91	92	93	94	95	96	97	98	99	100

2. Which number makes the problem true? (*Circle the correct letter.*)

$$12 + 4 = 7 + \underline{\qquad}$$

A. 6   **B.** 7   **C.** 8   **D.** 9

DAILY Warm-Up 28

Name _____ **Date** _____

1. Jane and Margaret want to make a necklace with beads. Jane has 12 beads. Margaret has 9 beads. Margaret's friend gives her 9 more beads. How many more beads must Jane get to have the same number of beads as Margaret? (*Circle the letter in front of the correct equation.*)

A. $12 + 9 = 9 + \underline{\qquad}$

B. $12 + \underline{\qquad} = 9 + 9$

C. $9 + \underline{\qquad} = 12 + 9$

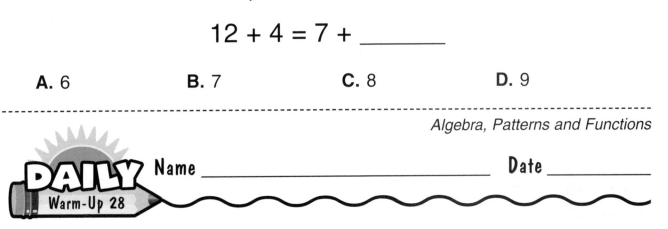

2. What is being done to the "IN" numbers to get to the "OUT" numbers?

_____

_____

_____

IN	OUT
8	6
6	4
4	2
2	0

DAILY Warm-Up 29

Name _____ Date _____

1. Complete the pattern below.

2, 6, 10, _____, _____, _____

2. Solve the problem.

2 + 4 = 6 + ☐

DAILY Warm-Up 30

Name _____ Date _____

1. Complete the chart. Write what pattern you see.

_____

_____

_____

NUMBER OF FINGERS			
1 person = **10** fingers		5 people = _____ fingers	
2 people = _____ fingers		6 people = _____ fingers	
3 people = _____ fingers		7 people = _____ ingers	
4 people = _____ fingers		8 people = _____ fingers	

2. Jack ran 3 laps on Monday, 6 laps on Tuesday, and 9 laps on Wednesday. If the pattern continues, how many laps will Jack run on Thursday? (*Circle the correct letter.*)

A. 6   **C.** 10

B. 8   **D.** 12

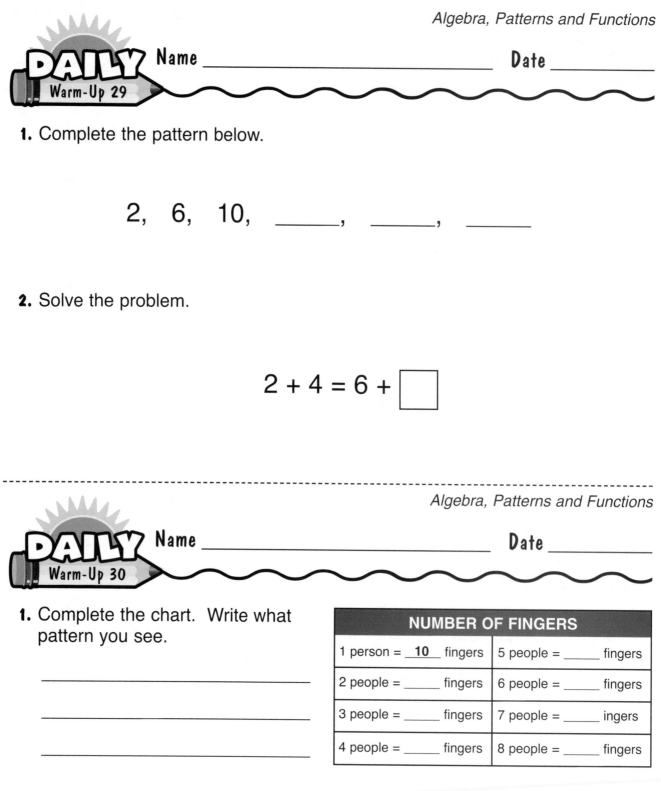

DAILY Warm-Up 31 **Name** _____ **Date** _____

1. Look at the bar graph. If the pattern of favorite animal continues, how many students will pick a dog as their favorite pet? (*Circle the correct letter.*)

A. 4 **B.** 6 **C.** 8

Student Favorite Animal

(bar graph: Frog = 2, Bird = 4, Cat = 6, Dog = blank; y-axis 0–10)

2. Solve the problems below.

A. $9 + 7 = 8 + \square$

B. $8 + 2 = 4 + \square$

C. $9 + 4 = 2 + \square$

D. $5 + 9 = 7 + \square$

E. $8 + 5 = 3 + \square$

F. $6 + 8 = 3 + \square$

G. $6 + 4 = 7 + \square$

H. $4 + 6 = 9 + \square$

I. $5 + 5 = 2 + \square$

DAILY Warm-Up 32 **Name** _____ **Date** _____

1. Look at the table below.

IN	2	3	4	5	6	7
OUT	3	4	5	6	7	8

What is being done to the "IN" numbers to get the "OUT" numbers?

_____

2. Answer the problems below.

IN	0	1	2	3	4	5
OUT	1	2	3	4	5	6

What is the rule?

_____

IN	4	5	6	7	8	9
OUT	2	3	4	5	6	7

What is the rule?

_____

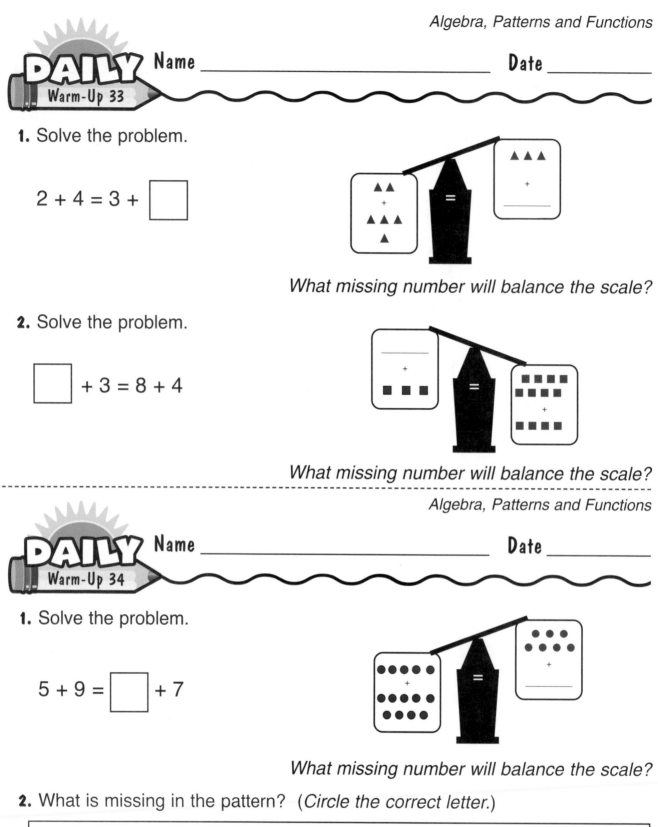

DAILY Warm-Up 33   Name _____   Date _____

1. Solve the problem.

$2 + 4 = 3 +$ ☐

What missing number will balance the scale?

2. Solve the problem.

☐ $+ 3 = 8 + 4$

What missing number will balance the scale?

DAILY Warm-Up 34   Name _____   Date _____

1. Solve the problem.

$5 + 9 =$ ☐ $+ 7$

What missing number will balance the scale?

2. What is missing in the pattern? (*Circle the correct letter.*)

A.   **B.**   **C.**

DAILY
Warm-Up 35

Name _____ Date _____

1. Use these shapes to make an **AABCAABC** pattern.

____ ____ ____ ____ ____ ____ ____ ____

2. Write four number sentences using 5, 4, and 9.

_____ + _____ = _____   _____ − _____ = _____

_____ + _____ = _____   _____ − _____ = _____

DAILY
Warm-Up 36

Name _____ Date _____

1. Write four number sentences about the shapes.

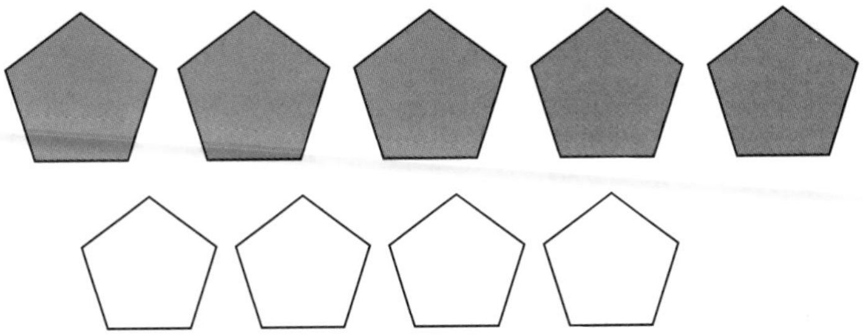

_____ + _____ = _____

_____ + _____ = _____

_____ − _____ = _____

_____ − _____ = _____

2. Draw an **ABCABC** pattern.

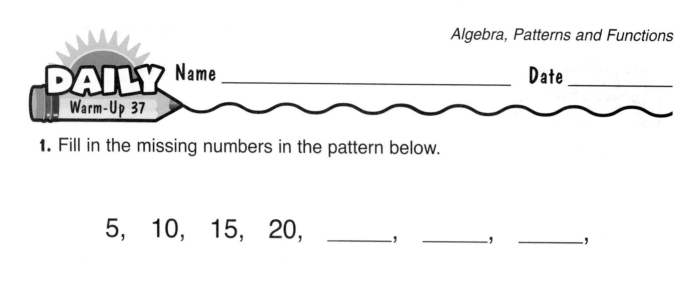

DAILY Warm-Up 37

Name _____ Date _____

1. Fill in the missing numbers in the pattern below.

5, 10, 15, 20, _____, _____, _____,

2. Jack wrote a pattern of numbers on paper. Complete Jack's pattern.

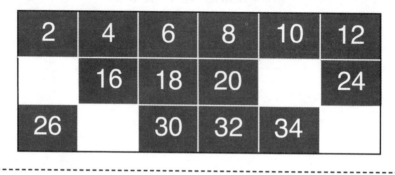

2	4	6	8	10	12
16	18	20		24
26		30	32	34	

DAILY Warm-Up 38

Name _____ Date _____

1. Continue the pattern below.

9, 12, 15, 18, _____, _____, _____

2. Continue the pattern of numbers in the boxes below.

| 5 | 8 | | 14 | 17 | 20 | | |

DAILY
Warm-Up 39

Name _____   **Date** _____

1. Write the missing numbers in the boxes below.

A. 7 + 4 = 6 + ☐   **D.** 5 + 6 = 4 + ☐   **G.** 1 + 2 = 3 + ☐

B. 8 + 3 = 5 + ☐   **E.** 6 + 8 = 9 + ☐   **H.** 4 + 8 = 9 + ☐

C. 8 + 5 = 3 + ☐   **F.** 3 + 4 = 5 + ☐   **I.** 8 + 6 = 5 + ☐

2. Jim has numbered squares lined up in this order: one, two, three, one, one, two, three, and three. He repeated the pattern again and lined up the squares until he reached 15 squares. How many number 2 squares did he have? (*Draw out numbered squares to act it out.*)

DAILY
Warm-Up 40

Name _____   **Date** _____

1. What is being done to the "IN" numbers to get the "OUT" numbers?

IN	5	6	7	8	9	10
OUT	10	11	12	13	14	15

_____

_____

2. Answer the problems below.

A. 6 + 4 = 9 + ☐   **D.** 5 + 7 = 6 + ☐   **G.** 5 + 3 = 6 + ☐

B. 9 + 8 = 5 + ☐   **E.** 8 + 8 = 9 + ☐   **H.** 6 + 8 = 9 + ☐

C. 8 + 5 = 3 + ☐   **F.** 6 + 6 = 5 + ☐   **I.** 1 + 4 = 5 + ☐

Name _____   **Date** _____

Warm-Up 41

1. Andrea mowed lawns this week. On Monday she mowed 2 lawns. On Tuesday she mowed 4 lawns. On Wednesday she mowed 6 lawns. If the pattern continues, how many lawns will Andrea mow on Thursday? *(Write your answer on the line.)*

_____ lawns

2. Write the rule of the table below.

IN	2	4	6	8
OUT	0	2	4	6

Rule: _____

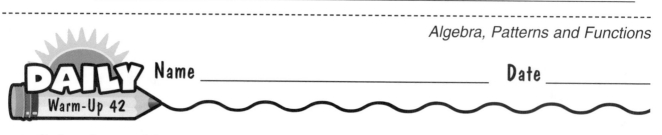

Name _____   **Date** _____

Warm-Up 42

1. Solve the problem.

$$3 + \boxed{} = 5 + 6$$

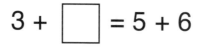

2. If the pattern of squares continues, how many squares will be in the 5th pattern? *(Circle the correct letter.)*

A. 5

B. 10

C. 15

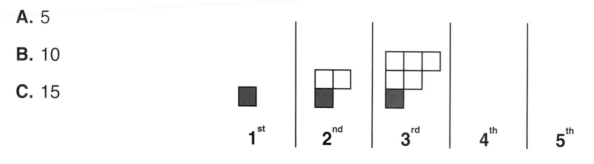

DAILY Warm-Up 43

Name _____ Date _____

1. Look at the pattern on the hundred chart. Use your pencil to shade in the rest of the pattern.

What is the pattern doing?

_____

_____

_____

1	2	3	4	5	6	7	8	9	10
11	12	13	14	15	16	17	18	19	20
21	22	23	24	25	26	27	28	29	30
31	32	33	34	35	36	37	38	39	40
41	42	43	44	45	46	47	48	49	50
51	52	53	54	55	56	57	58	59	60
61	62	63	64	65	66	67	68	69	70
71	72	73	74	75	76	77	78	79	80
81	82	83	84	85	86	87	88	89	90
91	92	93	94	95	96	97	98	99	100

2. Write the number that makes the problem true.

$$23 + 8 = 7 + \underline{\qquad}$$

DAILY Warm-Up 44

Name _____ Date _____

1. Use the shapes to create four number sentences.

_____ + _____ = _____

_____ + _____ = _____

_____ − _____ = _____

_____ − _____ = _____

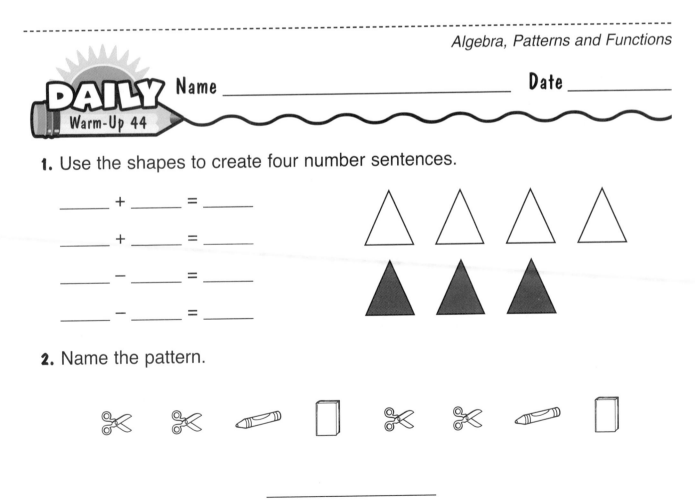

2. Name the pattern.

_____

Name _____ **Date** _____

DAILY Warm-Up 45

1. Fill in the missing numbers to the problems below.

A. $2 + 5 = 6 + \boxed{}$ **B.** $\boxed{} + 3 = 9 + 5$ **C.** $8 + \boxed{} = 4 + 9$

2. For each "A" Jake receives on his report card, his parents give him $2. Use the chart to find how much money Jake receives if he earns 5 "A's."

Money Jake Earned from His Report Card

"A's"	1	2	3	4	5
Money	$2	$4	$6	$8	

Name _____ **Date** _____

DAILY Warm-Up 46

1. Presley is making a bracelet out of numbered beads. What bead comes next in the numbered pattern? (*Circle the correct letter.*)

A. **2**

B. **3**

C. **4**

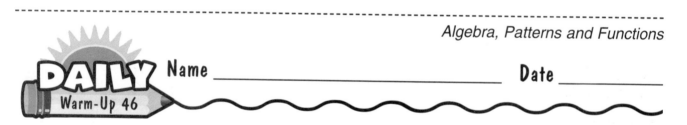

2. Diana has a suitcase of blocks. Which pattern can she make using only 6 blocks? (*Circle the correct letter.*)

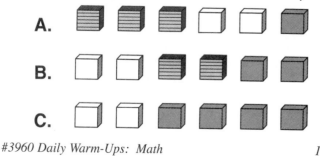

A.

B.

C.

DAILY Warm-Up 47

Name _____ **Date** _____

1. Which card would be next in the pattern? *(Circle the correct letter.)*

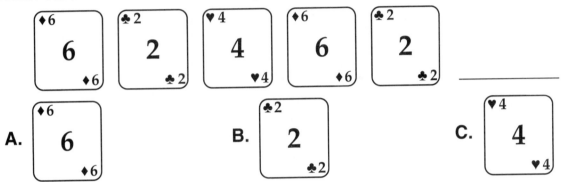

A. ♦6 6 ♦6   **B.** ♣2 2 ♣2   **C.** ♥4 4 ♥4

2. Write what number makes the problem true.

$$9 + \boxed{} = 7 + 14$$

DAILY Warm-Up 48

Name _____ **Date** _____

1. What's happening to the numbers in the "IN" column to get the numbers in the "OUT" column?

IN	10	9	8	7	6	5
OUT	7	6	5	4	3	2

_____

_____

2. Continue the pattern of numbers in the boxes below.

3	5	7	9		13	15	

DAILY Warm-Up 49

Name _____ Date _____

1. Which card would be next in the pattern? *(Circle the correct letter.)*

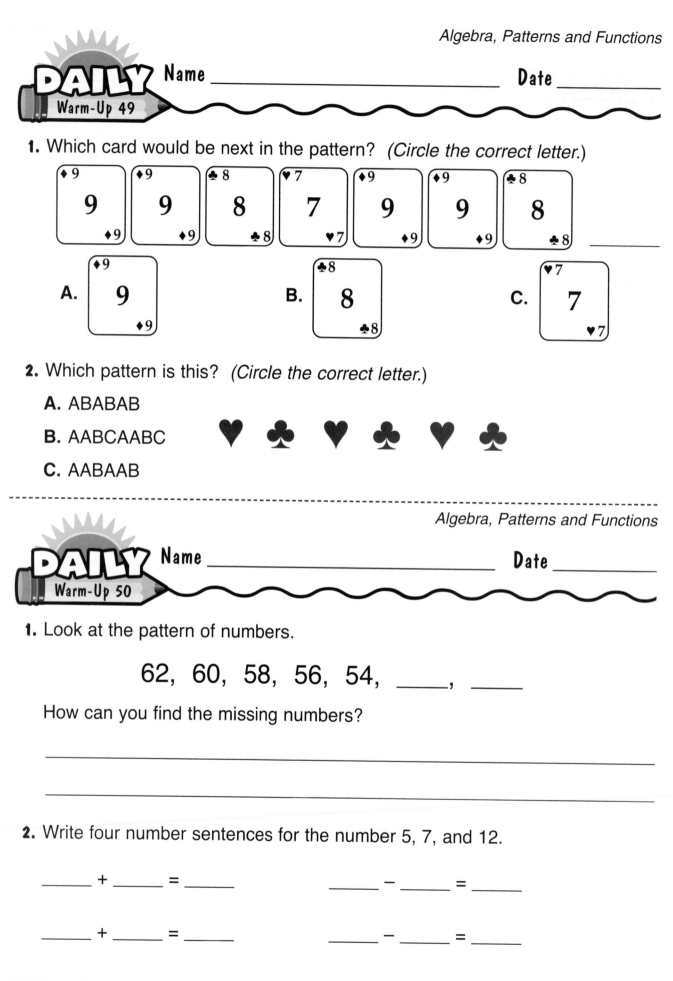

A. 9

B. 8

C. 7

2. Which pattern is this? *(Circle the correct letter.)*

A. ABABAB

B. AABCAABC

C. AABAAB

DAILY Warm-Up 50

Name _____ Date _____

1. Look at the pattern of numbers.

62, 60, 58, 56, 54, _____, _____

How can you find the missing numbers?

_____

_____

2. Write four number sentences for the number 5, 7, and 12.

_____ + _____ = _____   _____ − _____ = _____

_____ + _____ = _____   _____ − _____ = _____

Name _____ **Date** _____

DAILY
Warm-Up 51

1. Look at the table. If the pattern continues, how many lawns will Raymond mow on Saturday? (*Fill in the box.*)

Lawns Mowed	
Wednesday	4
Thursday	6
Friday	8
Saturday	

2. What comes next in the pattern? (*Circle the correct letter.*)

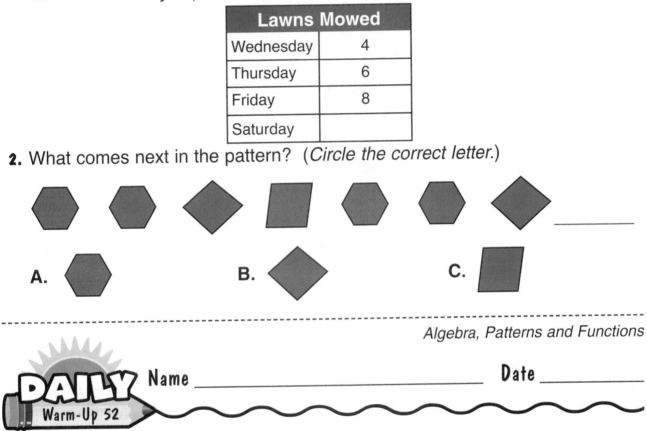

A.   B.   C.

Name _____ **Date** _____

DAILY
Warm-Up 52

1. Look at the pattern below. Which two shapes come next? (*Circle the correct letter.*)

A.

B.

C.

2. Solve the problem.

$$8 + z = 23$$

$$z = \underline{\quad\quad}$$

DAILY
Warm-Up 53

Name _____ Date _____

1. Look at the pattern of shaded numbers on the hundred chart. Explain what is being done.

1	2	3	4	5	6	7	8	9	10
11	12	13	14	15	16	17	18	19	20
21	22	23	24	25	26	27	28	29	30
31	32	33	34	35	36	37	38	39	40
41	42	43	44	45	46	47	48	49	50
51	52	53	54	55	56	57	58	59	60
61	62	63	64	65	66	67	68	69	70
71	72	73	74	75	76	77	78	79	80
81	82	83	84	85	86	87	88	89	90
91	92	93	94	95	96	97	98	99	100

_____

_____

_____

2. Which number makes the problem true? (*Circle the correct letter.*)

A. 6

B. 7

C. 8

D. 9

$$5 + 6 = 4 + \underline{\quad}$$

DAILY
Warm-Up 54

Name _____ Date _____

1. Fill in the missing number that makes the problem true.

$$16 + \underline{\quad} = 9 + 8$$

2. What is happening to the "IN" numbers to get the "OUT" numbers?

IN	4	6	8	10
OUT	8	10	12	14

_____

_____

DAILY Warm-Up 55

Name _____ Date _____

1. There are 10 napkins in a package and there are 25 students in our class. Each student needs one napkin. Which sentence shows how to find whether there are enough napkins? (*Circle the correct letter.*)

A. 10 – ____ = 25　　**B.** 10 + 25 = ____　　**C.** 25 – 10 = ____

2. For each chocolate cake Sarah bakes, she also bakes three strawberry cakes. If Sarah bakes five chocolate cakes, how many strawberry cakes will she bake? (*Fill in the box.*)

Chocolate Cakes	1	2	3	4	5
Strawberry Cakes	3	6	9	12	

DAILY Warm-Up 56

Name _____ Date _____

1. Finish the problem below. Write a story problem modeled by the numbers.

$$15 + \underline{\hspace{1cm}} = 24$$

_____

_____

_____

2. Look at the pattern of odd numbers. Circle the letter of the missing number that goes in the octagon.

A. 20

B. 21　　　15　17　19　◯　23　25

C. 23

DAILY Warm-Up 57

Name _____ Date _____

1. Look at the table. If the number 4 is put in, what number will come out? (*Circle the correct letter.*)

A. 6

B. 4

C. 2

IN	OUT
8	6
6	4
4	?
2	0

2. Explain what is being done to the numbers in the "IN" side to get the numbers in the "OUT" side?

_____

_____

_____

IN	OUT
1	4
2	5
3	6
5	8

DAILY Warm-Up 58

Name _____ Date _____

1. Fill in the missing number in the pattern.

4,   8,   12,   16,   ____ ,   24

2. Answer the problems below.

IN	0	1	2	3	4	5
OUT	3	4	5	6	7	8

What is the rule?

_____

_____

IN	2	3	4	5	6	7
OUT	3	4	5	6	7	8

What is the rule?

_____

_____

DAILY
Warm-Up 59

Name _____   Date _____

1. What shape goes in the empty space? (*Circle the correct letter.*)

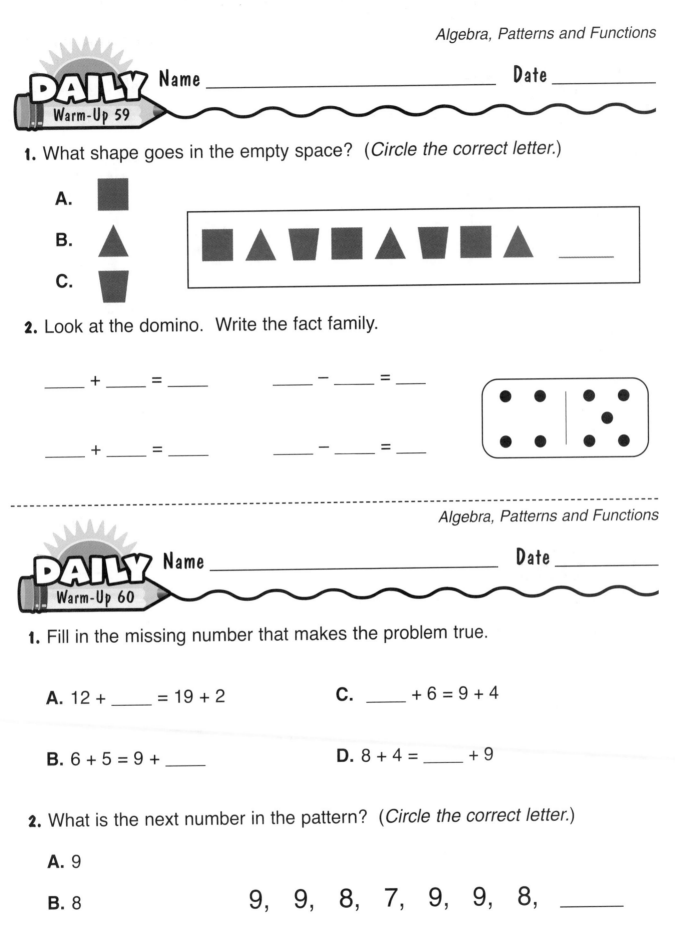

A. ■

B. ▲

C. ▼

2. Look at the domino. Write the fact family.

____ + ____ = ____   ____ – ____ = ____

____ + ____ = ____   ____ – ____ = ____

DAILY
Warm-Up 60

Name _____   Date _____

1. Fill in the missing number that makes the problem true.

A. $12 + \underline{\hspace{1cm}} = 19 + 2$

C. $\underline{\hspace{1cm}} + 6 = 9 + 4$

B. $6 + 5 = 9 + \underline{\hspace{1cm}}$

D. $8 + 4 = \underline{\hspace{1cm}} + 9$

2. What is the next number in the pattern? (*Circle the correct letter.*)

A. 9

B. 8

C. 7

9, 9, 8, 7, 9, 9, 8, _____

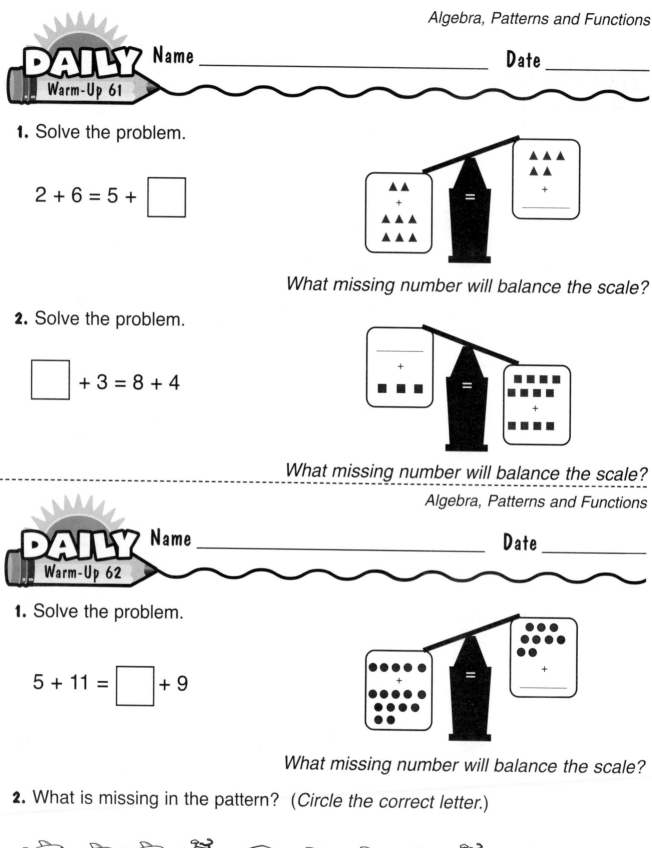

DAILY Warm-Up 61 Name _____ Date _____

1. Solve the problem.

$2 + 6 = 5 +$ ☐

What missing number will balance the scale?

2. Solve the problem.

☐ $+ 3 = 8 + 4$

What missing number will balance the scale?

DAILY Warm-Up 62 Name _____ Date _____

1. Solve the problem.

$5 + 11 =$ ☐ $+ 9$

What missing number will balance the scale?

2. What is missing in the pattern? (*Circle the correct letter.*)

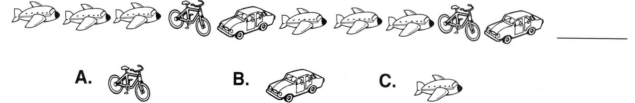

A. 🚲   **B.** 🚗   **C.** ✈

Warm-Up 1
1. 57, 58, 62
2. 10, 12, 14

Warm-Up 2
1. The pattern is decreasing by 1.
2. 18, 14, 12

Warm-Up 3
1. 20, 24, 28
2. Second Row: 35, 55
   Third Row: 70, 85, 90

Warm-Up 4
1. 17, 19, 21, 23
2. 9, 15, 21, 24

Warm-Up 5
1. 16, 18
2. B

Warm-Up 6
1. 18
2. 5, 9, 15

Warm-Up 7
1. 10
2. 5

Warm-Up 8
1. 5
2. 4, 8, 16

Warm-Up 9
1.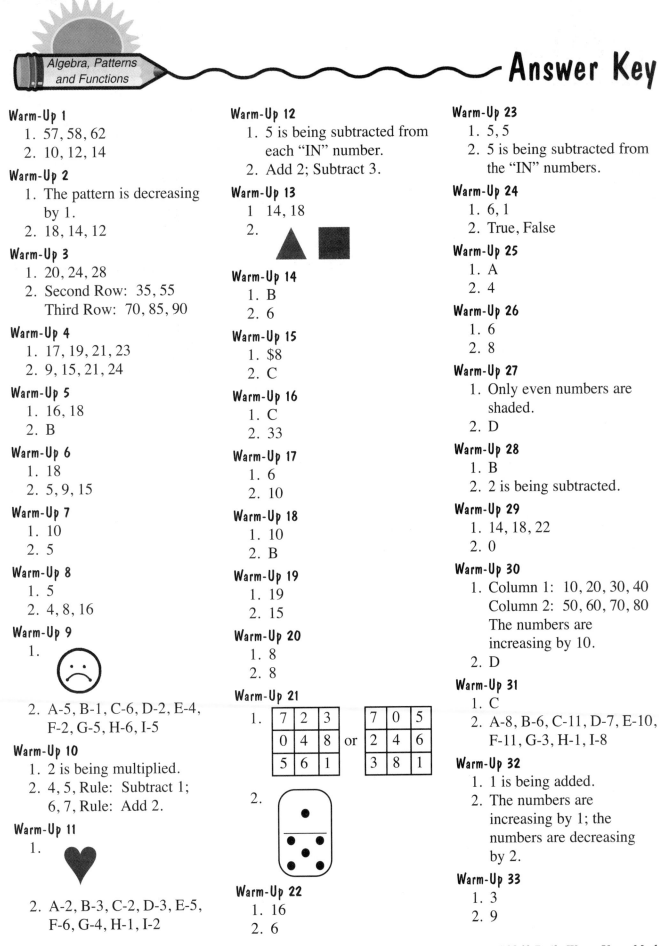
2. A-5, B-1, C-6, D-2, E-4, F-2, G-5, H-6, I-5

Warm-Up 10
1. 2 is being multiplied.
2. 4, 5, Rule: Subtract 1; 6, 7, Rule: Add 2.

Warm-Up 11
1.
2. A-2, B-3, C-2, D-3, E-5, F-6, G-4, H-1, I-2

Warm-Up 12
1. 5 is being subtracted from each "IN" number.
2. Add 2; Subtract 3.

Warm-Up 13
1. 14, 18
2.

Warm-Up 14
1. B
2. 6

Warm-Up 15
1. $8
2. C

Warm-Up 16
1. C
2. 33

Warm-Up 17
1. 6
2. 10

Warm-Up 18
1. 10
2. B

Warm-Up 19
1. 19
2. 15

Warm-Up 20
1. 8
2. 8

Warm-Up 21
1.

7	2	3
0	4	8
5	6	1

or

7	0	5
2	4	6
3	8	1

2.

Warm-Up 22
1. 16
2. 6

Warm-Up 23
1. 5, 5
2. 5 is being subtracted from the "IN" numbers.

Warm-Up 24
1. 6, 1
2. True, False

Warm-Up 25
1. A
2. 4

Warm-Up 26
1. 6
2. 8

Warm-Up 27
1. Only even numbers are shaded.
2. D

Warm-Up 28
1. B
2. 2 is being subtracted.

Warm-Up 29
1. 14, 18, 22
2. 0

Warm-Up 30
1. Column 1: 10, 20, 30, 40
   Column 2: 50, 60, 70, 80
   The numbers are increasing by 10.
2. D

Warm-Up 31
1. C
2. A-8, B-6, C-11, D-7, E-10, F-11, G-3, H-1, I-8

Warm-Up 32
1. 1 is being added.
2. The numbers are increasing by 1; the numbers are decreasing by 2.

Warm-Up 33
1. 3
2. 9

Answer Key

Warm-Up 34
1. 7
2. A

Warm-Up 35
1. Answers will vary.
2. 5 + 4 = 9
   4 + 5 = 9
   9 − 4 = 5
   9 − 5 = 4

Warm-Up 36
1. 5 + 4 = 9
   4 + 5 = 9
   9 − 4 = 5
   9 − 5 = 4
2. Answers will vary.

Warm-Up 37
1. 25, 30, 35
2. Second Row: 14, 22
   Third Row: 28, 36

Warm-Up 38
1. 21, 24, 27
2. 11, 23, 26

Warm-Up 39
1. A-5, B-6, C-10, D-7, E-5,
   F-2, G-0, H-3, I-9
2. 4

Warm-Up 40
1. 5 is being added
2. A-1, B-12, C-10, D-6, E-7,
   F-7, G-2, H-5, I-0

Warm-Up 41
1. 8
2. Two is subtracted from
   each "IN" number.

Warm-Up 42
1. 8
2. C

Warm-Up 43
1. Only odd numbers are
   being shaded.
2. 24

Warm-Up 44
1. 4 + 3 = 7, 3 + 4 = 7,
   7 − 3 = 4, 7 − 4 = 3
2. AABC

Warm-Up 45
1. A-1, B-11, C-5
2. $10

Warm-Up 46
1. B
2. B

Warm-Up 47
1. C
2. 12

Warm-Up 48
1. Three is being subtracted
   from the "IN" numbers.
2. 11, 17

Warm-Up 49
1. C
2. A

Warm-Up 50
1. 52, 50; Subtract 2 from
   each number to find
   missing numbers.
2. 5 + 7 = 12, 7 + 5 = 12,
   12 − 5 = 7, 12 − 7 = 5

Warm-Up 51
1. 10
2. C

Warm-Up 52
1. C
2. 15

Warm-Up 53
1. The pattern is counting by
   5s.
2. B

Warm-Up 54
1. 1
2. Four is being added to the
   "IN" numbers.

Warm-Up 55
1. C

2. 15

Warm-Up 56
1. 9; Answers will vary.
2. B

Warm-Up 57
1. C
2. The number 3 is being
   added.

Warm-Up 58
1. 20
2. Add 3; Add 1.

Warm-Up 59
1. C
2. 4 + 5 = 9, 5 + 4 = 9,
   9 − 4 = 5, 9 − 5 = 4

Warm-Up 60
1. A-9, B-2, C-7, D-3
2. C

Warm-Up 61
1. 3
2. 9

Warm-Up 62
1. 7
2. C